The Toolmakers Airgun

The Toolmakers Airgun

Paul Betts

The Toolmakers Airgun

Copyright 2016 to Redd INK Press

ISBN: 978-0-9905687-7-3

No part of this publication may be reproduced, stored in a retrieval system, or transmitted in any form or by any means, electronic, mechanical, photocopying, recording or otherwise, without the prior permission of the Publisher.

INTRODUCTION

Airguns and their various designs has always been a thing of great interest to me, especially the English sporting type, that was made in the mid eighteen hundreds. Production of the butt reservoir airgun seemed to die out about 1900, the history book will tell you this type of airgun had been developed hundreds of years prior to then. They have always been a very expensive item, mainly because they were more difficult to manufacture, compared to powder powered weapons. The valve seals were made from leather or horn and required regular maintenance, I guess those factors coupled with the manual pumping would have accounted for their demise. The sleek looking butt reservoir layout is a naturally interesting design, in my humble opinion. I always wanted to own an original but they are quite rare, and still very expensive. Then I thought, should I find one that was affordable would it be safe to charge and use in the field. Pumping high pressure air into any antique pressure vessel would give me cause for great concern, it could result in serious damage to my purchase and probably serious damage to myself. I would have been considering this with each stroke of the pump, this was one of the main reasons why I started to think about designing something that I could construct myself. I wanted my action to be sleek simple and reliable, I wanted the delicate antique styling combined with modern day performance.

The pump up airgun was re-born in the late 1960's thanks to the inventive work of the late Mr. Joe Wilkins from Pinxton in Nottinghamshire. He developed the coil sprung valve striking mechanism together with the high pressure under barrel reservoir layout. His idea was adopted commercially, firstly to power dart firing tranquilizer guns. Soon-after the manufacturer refitted rifled pellet firing barrels; Instantly the recoilless field target air rifle was born. Most modern airgun makers are still working around Joe's original design idea. Mr. Wilkins Jnr. from Ripley Derbyshire is the manufacturer of the world renowned "Ripley" airguns.

The very early butt reservoir rifles were made by isolated craftsmen from all over Europe. Records show some makers to date back over 400 years, information on antique airguns was very scarce prior to t'internet. The only stuff I could find was various photos from old books and catalogues, nothing contained any detailed information about the actual mechanics of the actions. The pictures suggested the hidden mechanical designs were all different, all appeared to have the hammer style cocking system, and they must have been powered by flat leaf type springs. Some had internal mainsprings, some had them mounted externally. The really early ones must have been ramrod loading with a smooth bore, some of the later looking ones had rotary loading taps built into the action.

For me, the sleek appearance was most important. I wanted my design to have a hammer style cocking system, with the power source being a flat leaf spring. It should be compact reliable and safe, with the appearance of a traditional old gun. The antique reservoirs were charged with stirrup pumps, I read these would only generate about 7 or 800 P.S.I. if they were working perfectly. The number and power of shots per charge would depend on the makers mechanical settings. The striker in a modern airgun delivers a direct blow to the valve head. The weight of the hammer combined with the power of the spring that provides its momentum are key parts of the design. The harder the valve is struck, the more power/less shots you get. The action is basically a linear movement controlled by a trigger release mechanism, think of the coil sprung hammers on the pinball machines.

My photos suggested none of the antique guns operated on this principal, high tensile coil springs had not been developed way back then. It's fairly easy to understand how a leaf spring can provide power to a rotary hammer, it's fairly easy to imagine a trigger mechanism that will release a cocked hammer, think of the shotgun lock. An airgun valve requires a slightly heavier blow to knock it open, simply scaling the hammer and spring combination up to deliver a direct blow to a firing pin would work, but I thought the compact design idea would have to go out of the window. I thought it would be better if the hammer could snap to rest against a dead stop after the firing cycle. Most of the antique actions appeared to function in this way, so somehow rotary motion must be converted to linear, similar to a connecting rod on a crankshaft. The connecting rod would force the valve open on the firing stroke, but it would also want to force it open on the cocking stroke; thus a type of bell crank or trip lever must be employed. The design should also incorporate a bypass system, whereby the hammer can be de- cocked without opening the reservoir valve. Some of the antique actions had small levers on the side, I could only guess that was what they were for.

Using this design means the linear force generated must be more than capable of opening the valve. The mainspring must force the hammer to return to its dead stop, otherwise the valve would jamb open causing all the reservoir charge to escape. So now the reservoir pressure and valve design enter the field of play. The hammer should not be over heavy and the spring should not be over strong, this could cause the gun to jump; thus disturbing the aim. The pictures suggested that this type of airgun was simple and crude, in practice they are complicated and fascinating from an engineering point of view. Years after my first design ideas "Hills" of Sheffield introduced the hand operated high pressure pumps specially for the airgun market. These were four times more powerful than the very best of the antique pumps, this moved the goal posts in my favor. I now had a firm new stepping stone to work from, that being the easily achievable high pressure air. I could be positive with reservoir design and then re-work forward.

The problem.
Pipe ----- (barrel)
Bit in the middle ----- (action)
Bottle of high pressure air ----- (reservoir)

Design the bit in the middle; this must momentarily knock open the bottles valve causing a quick and powerful blast of the stored air to flow down the pipe. The pressure in the bottle should be as high as is practically achievable; the bit in the middle should be as compact in design as is practically achievable; it should not impair the aiming of the pipe during operation. You could give this job to twelve thousand capable engineers who were working in isolation; they all would come up with a design that would work; I am sure. Many would work fine but look wrong; many would look fine but work wrong. Some would arrive with a good combination, many probably far better than mine. But, I could guarantee; no two would look or operate exactly the same; of that I am certain. Sorting the above presents an enormous amount of different design permutations, and that's before considering the introduction of a suitable loading tap design into the equation.

I spent years building various prototypes and eventually crossed all the bridges mentioned earlier with great success. I based my design round a cam and spring loaded trip, so as to keep the action as compact as possible. Production required some delicate operations that had to be done on the milling machine, soon-after close inspection made me realize the large valve arrangement I had designed need only be knocked open very slightly, so as to provide an adequate blast. So; I straightway designed an action that would let the hammer deliver a direct blow to the firing pin. I felt certain that it would work provided the spring/hammer combination was correct, my main fear was that the inertia force created by the heavier hammers rotation would disturb the aim. Practical tests proved this was not to be a problem, because the hammers energy was absorbed by the opposing air pressure; unlike it snapping on to a dead stop. The action looked more sleek, it was easier to make and seemed to be more "air efficient" but the big bonus was that the new design required just a couple of very simple milling operations.

Developing anything mechanical usually requires a lot of patience, especially something of this nature. The action must function correctly and at the same time look reasonable, development in one area would often scrap improvements that had been made previously in other areas. On a project like this as you can work out; the slightest alteration would usually result in having to do a total action re- make. So because of this as time goes on, longer and longer periods of mental debate would precede any practical development work. Some ideas could only be developed after practical tests had been proven. If you should come up with an improved design, please write a book…. so I can try to copy.

The action has to be built in stages, so I decided to map the route for my own reference. The turning work on the action is quite basic apart from some lathe cut screw threads, these have to be formed on the valve and cylinder adapter. The bulk of the work is mainly accurate scribing sawing filing and drilling. No part of the action has been copied or adapted from other makers work; you won't find anything even similar in design or in style; in books or on t'internet. I have done my best to map the course. I do hope you can follow and enjoy, I am not a writer or a draughtsman.

I was a Ripley lad, and still live quite near, so I decided to present my efforts to Steve at "Ripley Rifles" He said the design was very good, and thought it to be totally unique. He had not seen or heard of any other butt reservoir type airgun (antique or modern) with a rotary hammer working on the "direct hit" principal. The action is designed to work within a reservoir pressure band, ranging from 100 to 150 BAR this is roughly 1500 to 2200 P.S.I. Provided this is observed the action should give good service for donkey's years.

In summary, the butt reservoir airgun was designed around four hundred years ago, probably for killing small game. By 1790 the design had been improved to a standard whereby good enough to equip the snipers in the Austrian military. These rifles shot large caliber lead balls; they were reported to have an effective range of up to 150 yards; they had a gravity fed tubular magazine, so they were capable of a rapid rate of fire. This, combined with them being smokeless made them a very serious tool; the manual pumping coupled with tedious maintenance work they required led to their demise after about 20 years of service.

From what I could work out, production of the sporting butt reservoir airgun continued until around 1900. Makers seemed to be scattered all over England; but they were scarce. The photographs seemed to suggest that by this time they were all working to a very similar design? most guns being supplied with both rifled and smooth bore barrels, pump and tools; all in a nice fitted leather case. They would have been very expensive way back then. Though capable of killing most soft skinned animals this type of gun was to become "I think" more of a rich gentleman's plaything or conversation piece………. Something to acquire and add to ones collection. The mass produced spring powered airguns were developed soon-after and became commonplace. The reservoir gun would lay dead for 70 years and then re-appear looking like a space invaders ray-gun. The sleek lines of the leaf sprung butt reservoir airgun is now only visible to most in the museums, history books, or……. on t'internet.

THE ACTION OVERVIEW

The mainframe or main part of the gun is produced from four pieces of bright drawn mild steel that are welded together - if the joints are filled goodly they will file up nicely and the welding work will be unseen.

The socket -------- the bit the reservoir valve screws into.
The plate --------- the central bit ---- which everything fits to.
The two lugs ----- these blank the end of the socket off and blend it to the plate.

I have always used the stick welder for the operations - the joints must be strong airtight and filled - the amps must be set correctly and the rod tip kept close so as not to cause undercut - if this part is sorted properly the shaping work is simple.

The sketch below shows how the parts fit together - firstly the lugs are welded to the plate then they are trued up and chamfered - ready for the radial weld - parts are produced so as to make perfect alignment simple.

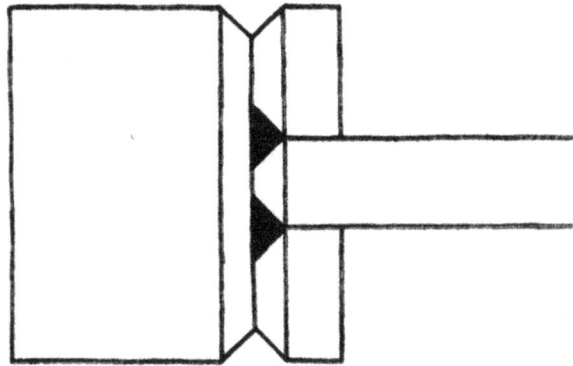

Bright drawn mild was my choice for all the parts - using anything more exotic may lead to problems - the heat from the welding work could result in hardening - this would make the filework and thread re-sizing very difficult - the natural surface finish on bright drawn mild is just right - as the finished job should look old - excessive polishing is not required on any of the parts - more important is that the mainframe plate is nice and flat.

The action is designed to fit to any common airgun barrel (rifled) up to 2·5 calibre - or a fabricated smooth bore barrel up to 16mm. O.D. and to produce 12 ft. lbs. energy.

The shapes and hole centers must be marked accurately - study the hints and tips page - remember this was a "hand made" project done mainly with "hand tools" so hand and eye coordination governs the quality and appearance of the finished product - study the sketches and the cover photograph - read the text - work out what each part is actually doing - this will help you understand just how accurate the part must be - think of the hand made knife - its outer shape is usually not so critical but the handle must be firm and it should be honed symmetrically - as you know - it only takes a few scratches or a slightly uneven edge to spoil its overall appearance.

The trigger mechanism is totally unique; it took me years to develop the basic idea. I have since studied t'internet and can find no reference whatsoever to any design that is even similar.

THE SOCKET

Firstly I made the socket so it could be used to gauge the threads on the valve - it is most important that the thread is of standard size - it must also be central and square (the end of the socket usually contracts slightly after it has been welded to the lugs - in that case the plug tap can be re-sunk so as to restore the thread to being standard) - a bright drawn mild steel blank is required 1-3/8" dia. x 1" long - study the sketch.

Set in the 3 jaw - face lightly - drill through so as to finish bore to ·820 (the same thread is formed in the cylinder adapter and pump adapter - so I turned a plug gauge to make inspection easy).

Set the lathe to cut the 5/8" B.S.P. thread (take care to stop just short of full depth - transfer to the vice - finish with a good sharp tap - use a good quality cutting compound so the thread is as smooth as possible - and of standard size).

Set the tap running true - screw the socket on so it locks up to the jaws - turn the O.D. to 1·260 (stop a few thou. short of the chuck jaws) - face lightly (stop a few thou. short of the tap flutes).

Re-set turned round gripping on the O.D. and running true - face to length - set the compound to cut the 45° weld prep. chamfer - study the sketch.

Re-set turned round and running true - cut a minimal 45° chamfer on the thread start - de-burr the outer corner (do not chamfer) - remove - clean thoroughly (old toothbrush - paraffin?) - store safely (later - the socket is fitted to the valve so as a slight taper can be turned on the O.D.).

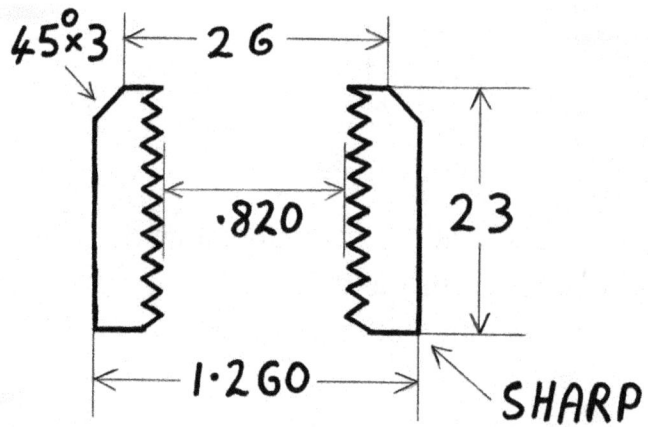

THE RESERVOIR VALVE

The valve is a simple unregulated "pea in a bottleneck type" - in the order of keeping the action small the hammer/spring combination must be delicate - yet it must be capable of knocking the valve open when the reservoir is fully charged - clearances are minimal so the parts should be accurate and concentric - study the sketch.

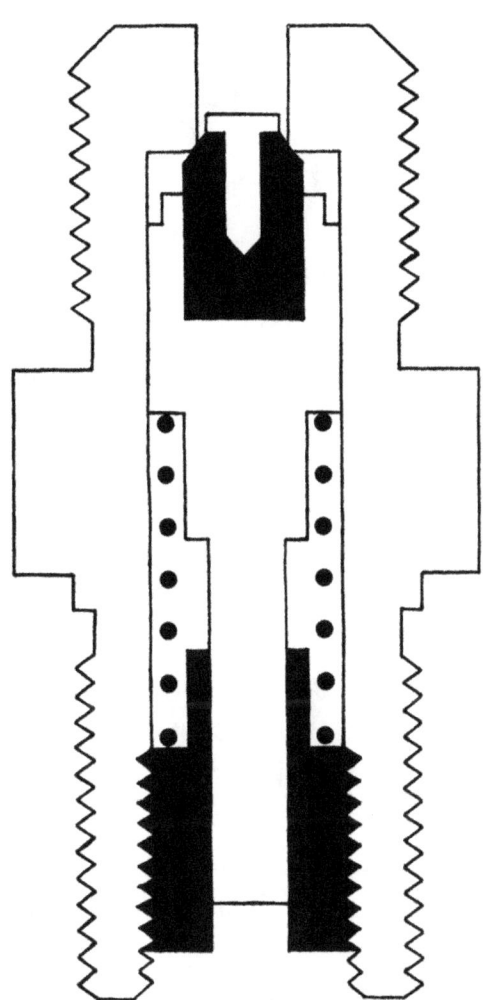

The valve is made from 1-1/4" dia. CZ 121 brass - this is a tough engineering grade alloy that is good to machine - a 2-1/2" long blank is required - dim's are in metric and imperial - study the sketch.

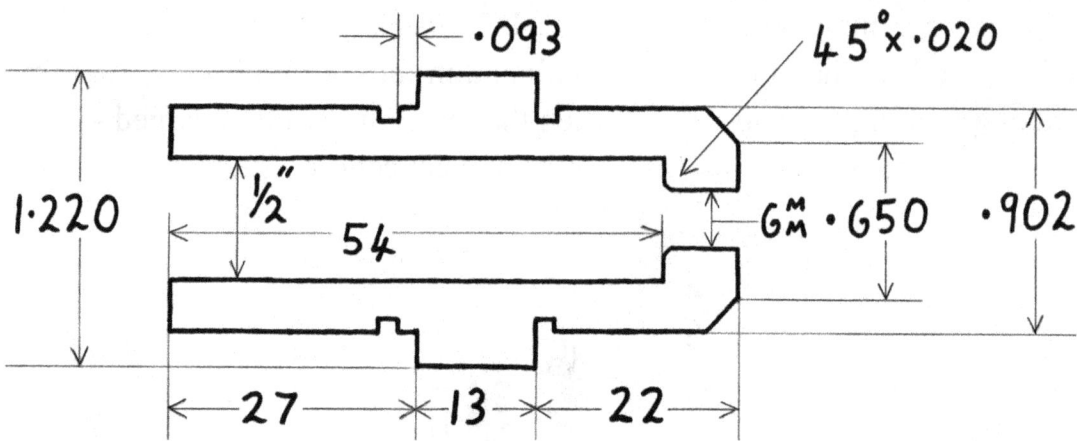

Set the blank in the 3 jaw - face lightly - turn the ·902 x 22mm. - turn the 1·220 up to the jaws (finish with fine emery - leave the outer corner sharp) - centerdrill - sink halfway through with a sharp 6mm. drill - study the sketch.

Turn round - set running true - turn the other ·902 so it leaves the 13mm. wide shoulder (again - sharp outer corner) - face so as to leave the total length at 62mm. - centerdrill - sink through with the 6mm. drill - study the sketch.

The spindle hole and valve seat must now be formed - select a good 1/2" drill - use the oilstone or diamond file to remove the sharp cutting edges (this prevents the drill from tearing or screwing itself into the brass it is most important when enlarging an existing hole) - it is called "negative rake"

Sink in slowly until the drill is cutting at full dia. then index in exactly 50mm. (use the carbide scriber to mark a visual depth stop on the upper drill flute?).

Grind the drill to form a flat bottom - sink in exactly 54mm. (again - carbide scribe mark - feed steadily) - study the sketch.

Re-grind to a 45° cutting angle so as to form the seat (use the square as a gauge - again - negative rake) - set the drill point close to the edge of the 6mm. hole - lock the tailstock - wind in gently so as to touch on (chuck stationery) - set a ·020 feeler against the valve end face so as to position a scribe mark on the upper drill flute - start the chuck (run slowly to avoid chatter - listen for the drill touching on) - sink in to the scribe mark - inspect with the torch - study the sketch.

Start a sharp 9/16" U.N.F. plug tap off in the 1/2" hole (guide in square with the tailstock center - do not go over 1/2" deep - use the fibre pen to mark the tap grooves for a visual depth stop - the thread is for the valve guide - it is cut to the correct depth - later).

Form the thread run out groove - it is 1/8" wide x ·050 deep (take care to leave the ·093 parallel land in the shoulder - it supports the O ring that makes the valve seal to the cylinder adapter - use the 3/32" drill shank to assist with aligning the tool) - study the sketch.

Turn round set running true - cut the other thread run out groove (this one is hard up to the shoulder) - study the sketch.

Set the lathe to cut the 5/8" B.S.P. thread (this thread needs to be slightly oversize the reservoir should not feel sloppy when it's attached to the action - use the socket to gauge the thread to be of minimal clearance - ensure the threads are cleaned thoroughly before inspection - old toothbrush?).

Set to cut the adapter thread (this thread should be of standard size - not sloppy - not tight - inspect with the socket - again - clean thoroughly before testing) - when all is well set the compound to cut a minimal 45° chamfer on the internal and external thread starts.

Turn round set running true - set the compound to cut the larger thread start - this should run out at about ·650 on the face - study the sketch - polish the face with wet/dry (the Dowty washer in the pump adapter has to seal here).

At this point a suitable stainless steel spring must be found that will force the valve to close - then the guide and spindle can be made - study the assembly sketch - it should be about 25mm. long and 8mm. I.D. - the one I used was made from ·050 dia. wire - so you can imagine it need not be super strong.

Produce a 9/16" U.N.F. test nut (brass off-cut?) - set the lathe to screwcut about 1" of CZ 121 brass to be a nice fit in the nut - face - turn the 8mm. spring location stalk - cut a minimal 45° chamfer on the thread start - saw/part so as to leave 14mm. of the thread - study the sketch.

Grip on the stalk - face the thread to finished length - cut a minimal 45° chamfer on the thread start - transfer to the vice - use the edge of a small warding file to cut a nice sharp screwdriver slot across the end face (about 1/16" wide x 1/16" deep) - study the sketch.

Tap the valve thread to depth - the guide should screw in and lock up when its end face is about 3mm. lower than the valves end face (set in the vices soft jaws - avoid overtapping - take care with this - study the assembly sketch).

Lock the guide in the valve (grind an old chisel to make a driver?) - set the assembly running true - centerdrill - drill 4·7mm. - ream 5mm. - remove - de-burr (now the valve spindle should fit central and square).

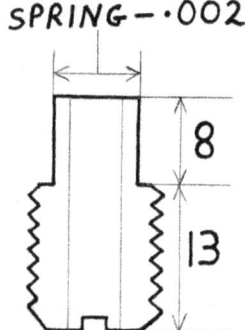
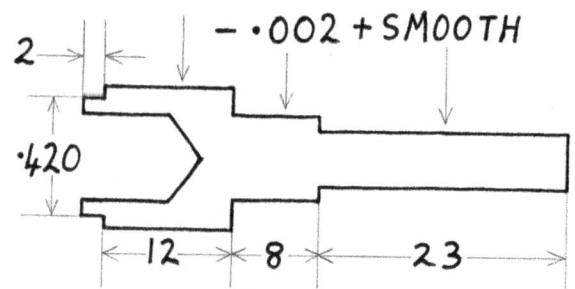

The valve spindle is made from stainless steel - rough turn the tail to ·210 dia. - face - center with a small centerdrill - set further out and up to the revolving tailstock centre to rough turn the spring stalk and larger dia. - study the sketch.

Note the exact dia. of the guides reamed hole - the spring I.D. - and the drilled hole in the valve - now finish all dia's so as the spindle has ·002 clearance - use a tool that will leave a nice finish and sharp corner - (allow for finishing with fine emery - study the sketch).

Grip on the spring stalk - set running true - face to total length - turn the ·420 x 2mm. - centerdrill - select a nice sharp 5/16" drill - sink in steadily until the point is cutting at full dia. then index in 8mm. - study the sketch.

Gauge the holes exact dia. then produce the nylon blank - it should be ·001 larger than the hole - it should be about 13mm. long - with faced ends.

Press the blank in the spindle (bottomed) - grip on the spring stalk - set the assembly running true - face so as 4mm. protrudes - centerdrill (tiny) - drill 2·5mm. x 1/4" deep - de-burr with the scalpel point - inspect with the loupe.

Set the compound to cut the 45° sealing angle - the finish should be smooth and it should leave a 5mm. flat on the front face (use a razor sharp tool - inspect with the loupe) - study the assembly sketch.

Produce the end cap for the firing pin to push on (this should be slightly tougher than mild steel - use an old drill shank - or allen screw shank?) - the stalk should be 6mm. long - it should be ·001 bigger than the hole in the nylon - the head should be 5mm. dia. - it should be faced to ·050 thick and de-burred - study the assembly sketch.

Now three equi-spaced flats must be filed on the large dia. - set the lathe in low gear - grip on the tail - set one jaw dead vertical - file the flat so it is square to the jaw and parallel with the dia. - work down so as to touch onto the ·420 dia. - rotate - repeat - de-burr thoroughly with the needle file - inspect closely.

Clean the parts thoroughly - assemble - grip in the chuck so as to push on the end cap with a small drift or screwdriver - check it opens and closes smoothly (later - a blind drive peg hole is drilled in the shoulder) - an O ring that is about 1" O.D. x ·072 thick is now required (see materials).

You may be thinking that the valve design will restrict the blast - as you can see there is only a couple of thou. clearance between the spindle and the guide - you may be thinking that a series of flats grooves or holes around the spindle would assist - don't be fooled ---- the small amount of air that is trapped in the valve will provide for a more than adequate blast.

THE RESERVOIR

The reservoirs on the antique airguns were usually of a conical shape - they were constructed from rolled iron sheet - the seams were riveted then made airtight with braze or solder then they were covered with a layer of thin leather or sharkskin - this was so they were not cold to the touch - this was the most practical way to produce an airtight vessel way back then - for safety reasons this construction method should be left on the shelf hidden away in the history book.

The under-barrel reservoirs on the modern airguns are usually made from non ferrous seamless tubing - they are pressure tested to withstand twice there routine working pressure before they are used in operation.

The S.W.P. ----- Safe Working Pressure ---- is usually indent stamped or engraved into their construction so there is no confusion when they are charged some manufacturers make actions that work on a charge pressure of about 2200 P.S.I. --- or --- Pounds per. Square Inch --- others make them to work on about 3300 P.S.I. this is mainly about getting more shots per. charge rather than the power level - the power of the air blast is governed by the valve/striker design together-with the size of the airway that leads to the breech - airguns must be manufactured so they do not exceed the legal power limit which is set for air powered weapons here in the U.K. (more on this subject - later).

The early "modern" airguns were all charged by de-canting the air from a large diver's tank - since then "Hills" of Sheffield developed the hand operated high pressure air pump especially for the airgun market - the company have been manufacturing various types of pumps since 1841 - they are capable of charging the under barrel reservoirs to 3300 P.S.I. as most of them are quite low in volume - all my early prototypes were developed with a homemade cylinder - for safety reasons - we will not go down that road.

Some of the very latest airguns that work on 3300 P.S.I. use a miniature diver's type cylinder for the reservoir - these also attach under the barrel - because these are greater in volume they have to be filled with the de-canting method - it is a similar type cylinder that is best suited to this application - luckily the maximum charge pressure required for this project is only 2200 P.S.I. - so the pump is ideal - they have a built in gauge so the charge pressure is precise - if set correctly the action should provide a shot for each stroke of the pump.

The cylinder that is best suited for this application is referred to as an aluminium buddy bottle - the one required is manufactured by a company called Luxfer - this type of cylinder is an accessory carried by divers - they hold a small amount of air that can be used in an emergency - they are also used for inflating a B.C.D. Buoyancy Control Device - this is an inflatable vest - they have a tailored compartment that the cylinder fits in - these cylinders are tested to withstand 348 BAR. or just over 5000 P.S.I.

There are many makes of buddy bottle - some are made of steel - some have a tapered thread in the neck (THESE ARE NOT SUITABLE).

The one required is about 9-5/8" long (without valve) - the body is about 2-3/8" O.D. and the neck is just under 1-1/4" O.D. - the thread is M.18 x 1·5 and parallel - there is an O ring counterbore in the neck face so they can lock and seal to a square shoulder - this size cylinder comes in two styles one has a flat base (it will stand vertical on a flat surface) - the other has a slightly rounded base (these will not stand vertical).

The one with the rounded base is more suitable for this application - it should be in good condition - general paint flaking is not a problem but I rejected anything that looked abused or bashed about.

Remove the valve (hold tightly - tap the A clamp with the mallet) - inspect the thread closely - see it is crisp and sharp - see it is clean and corrosion free internally - if all is well prepare as below.

Scrape any flaking paint off with the scalpel - use the needle file to remove any swelling that may have occurred around the indent stamping - see the neck face is burr free and clean - obtain a new O ring - store the cylinder and the O ring safely.

THE CYLINDER ADAPTER

The cylinder adapter is made from CZ 121 brass - or a stainless steel that is not to tough to machine easily - a 1-1/4" dia. x 3-1/16" long blank is required.

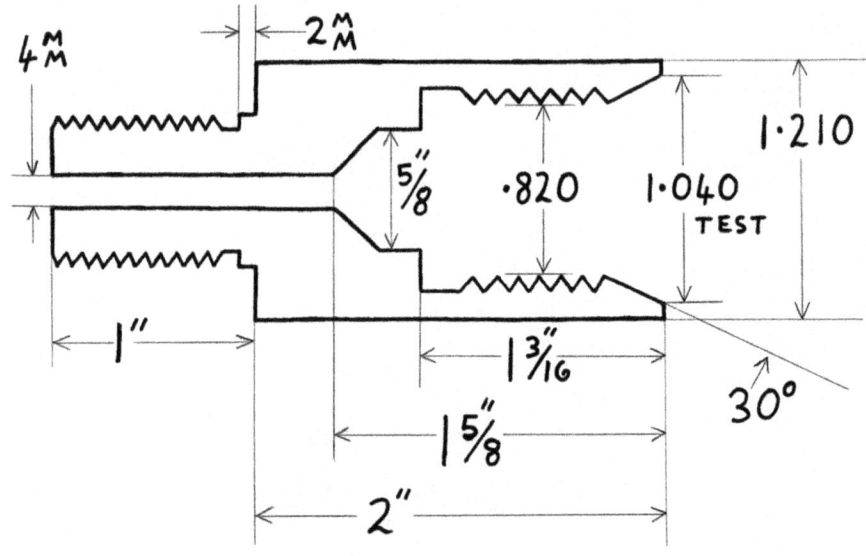

Set in the 3 jaw - face - turn the 1·210 up to the jaws.

Turn round set running true - face to length - turn the ·709 x 1"

Form the thread run-out groove - it is ·050 deep (use the 2mm. drill shank to gauge the shoulder land) - study the sketch.

Set the lathe to cut the M.18 x 1·5 thread - this should have standard clearance - inspect with the reservoir (great care is needed here - aluminium threads "pick up" or "gall" easily - clean thoroughly - lubricate with a drop of silicone oil before inspection - feel for clearance - remove and re-cut if seeming at all tight).

When all is well cut a minimal 45° chamfer on the thread start.

Turn round set running true - centerdrill - set the 5/8" drill point level with the face then sink in 1-5/8" - set the 20mm. drill point level with the face then sink in 1-1/16" - bore so as to form the ·820 x 1-3/16" (plug gauge) - study the sketch.

Form the thread run-out groove (this can be up to 3/16" wide) x ·050 deep.

Set the lathe to cut the 5/8" B.S.P. thread (this should be of standard size - not sloppy - not tight - inspect with the valve).

Fit the O ring to the valve - set the compound to cut the seal taper (this should run out at about 1·040 on the face - the O ring should start to trap when the valves shoulder is about 20 thou. away from locking up) - see the threads are clean and see the tapers finish is smooth - fit to test when near - the outer corner should be sharp and burr-free - study the sketch.

Turn round set running true - centerdrill - drill through 4mm. - remove - de-burr.

Wash the cylinder out with hot soapy water - rinse and let dry - clean the adapter thoroughly - fit the O ring in the cylinder counterbore - put a small smear of silicone grease on the threads (silicone grease is not pressure explosive) --------

NEVER USE ANY OIL BASED GREASES ----- THESE WILL EXPLODE.

Assemble hand tight - store safely (soon the necessary equipment is produced for locking the parts together - so they are all good and tight.

Later - the cylinder and adapter is primed and painted - the valve shoulder is a few thou. larger than the adapters O.D. - this provides a sharp edge to work up to - and it protects the end of the coating.

THE PUMP ADAPTER

Most pump hoses usually end with a 1/8" B.S.P. female thread - so a 1/8" male to male connector and two 1/8" Dowty washers are required (see materials) - the adapter is best made from 1-1/4" dia. CZ 121 brass - a 1-1/4" long blank is required - study the sketch.

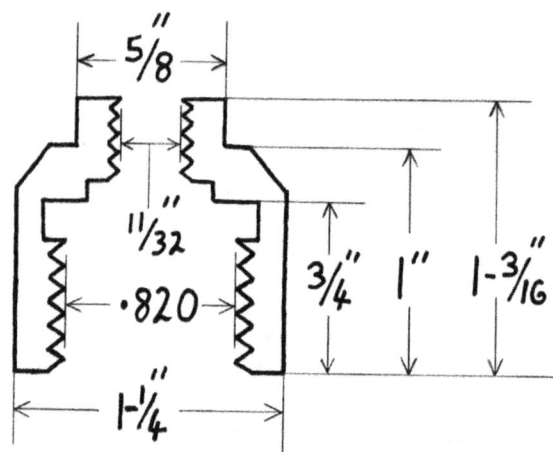

Set in the 3 jaw running true - face - centerdrill - drill through 11/32" - set the 20mm. drill point level with the face then sink in 3/4" (negative rake).

Bore out to ·820 x 3/4" deep (plug gauge) - form the thread run-out undercut (it can be up to 1/4" wide x ·050 deep) - set the lathe to cut the thread (standard size - inspect with the valve) - cut a minimal 45° chamfer on the thread start.

Form the counterbore that locates the Dowty washer - this should be ·010 clearance on the washers O.D. - the face should be smooth so the washer will seal - the depth must allow the washers face to protrude so as it will trap and seal on the valve face (fit the washer on the end of a pencil - align to inspect).

Turn round set running true - face to length - form the 5/8" stalk - tap through 1/8" B.S.P. (set square with tailstock center) - form a small 45° chamfer on the thread start - form the large outer chamfer - study the sketch - remove - clean thoroughly.

Fit the male to male connector to the stalk (trapping the other Dowty) - lock on the pump hose (the Dowty washers are cleverly designed to let the gas or fluid pressure force the flexible skirts hard up to the joint faces - hence the adapter need only be hand tight when fitted to the valve - no need for any spanner flats).

TESTING AND FINISHING

I can only recommend the pump fill for this application - the bulk tank de-cant method is awkward to control precisely - I can recommend the pumps made by "Hills" they are well made and perfect for the job - they come complete with an accurate pressure gauge and fill hose - you can deal with the company direct - the factory is in Halfway - South East Sheffield.

Now - assembly/disassembly without causing damage to the parts (this is what I did) - produce an aluminium v block about 7/8" thick - study the sketch (this is used with an aluminium jaw protector - so as to grip the reservoir adapter in the vice (solid area - just below valve thread) without causing any serious damage.

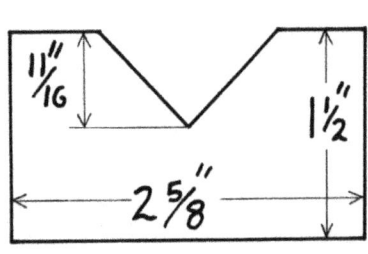 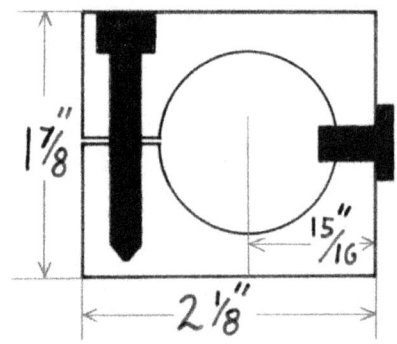

Now use the large Gordon grips to lock the reservoir onto the adapter (grip in the neck area - use a narrow strip of stout leather belting to protect the cylinder from the sharp jaw serrations).

Now the valve must be locked into the adapter - I did not have any pin wrenches - they are quite expensive and I was not certain that they would do the job (this is what I did) - produce a 12mm. thick blank - study the sketch (I used ground flat stock but brass or mild steel would do the same) - set the blank in the 4 jaw to square the edges up and then drill/bore the 1·220 - the hole should be parallel - smooth de-burred and ·001 clearance on the valve shoulder - study the sketch.

Drill/ream for the 6mm. drive pin (central in the face) - drill/tap for the clamping screw (M.6) - form the slit with the hacksaw - de-burr - clean - clamp the plate to the valve (central on the shoulder) - set the assembly in the drill vice so as to drill the pin hole (set the depth stop so as the drill point stops inline with the bottom of the thread run out groove).

Turn the headed drive pin (old allen screw shank? - it should enter into the shoulder by about 4mm.) - study the sketch - the plate clamps to the valve so it cannot wobble about - the bore is smooth and the pin is close fitting (now the valve can be locked in with the Gordon grips - or similar - without causing any serious damage to the parts).

At this point fit the socket to the valve - set running true - so as to turn a slight taper on the socket O.D. - it should start at about 1·225 (5 thou. larger than the valve shoulder - it should run out at the start of the weld prep. chamfer - the finish need not be polished - as this area is finished with the file/needlefile later - the angle is just over 1° - take care here).

Use the centerpop to mark the weld prep. chamfer inline with the drive pin hole (this is a setting aid - for when the welding work is done) - remove.

Ensure parts are thoroughly clean for test assembly - apply a tiny smear of silicone grease to the thread and O ring before locking up.

Hold the pump adapter facing upwards - drop the Dowty washer in - see it is settled in the counterbore - screw the reservoir down (hand tight) - charge to 50 BAR - hold the cylinder vertical - use a hammer and small drift to tap the valve open - if all is well there should be a sharp blast (proving pressure exists).

Charge to 150 BAR - immerse in clear water - look closely - be certain that the O rings are sealing and the valve is shutting off - if all is not well make adjustments now (get this sorted proper and the reservoir will hold pressure ------ for years).

To discharge the reservoir - produce a 5mm. dia. spacer bar with faced ends (about 10mm. long) - use the connector so as to jack the valve open (go steady with this operation - let the air escape very slowly).

Now for one of the most difficult stages of the entire project ------

Heron - I could only think of de-greasing with hot soapy water or methylated spirit and then priming with acid etch primer (Landrover body stuff) - then finishing with a matte finish dark brown/ish or black/ish paint (the main objective being to get some dark/ish colour plastered on that would bond to the cylinder and adapter - blobs blotches streaks and runs being totally unimportant).

HINTS AND TIPS

To produce the mainframe and all the parts that fit to it, accurate scribing grinding filing and drilling is essential. Here are a few tips that may assist with production.

Grinding/filing - only work in good light, if you can't see the line, you can't work to it. Check the grinders tool rest is set correctly, so as the wheel will not undercut the scribe. Keep scribers fine and sharp. See the work vice is mounted firmly, if careful, it is possible to virtually file a scribed line in half. Only use sharp files, have a stiff wire brush or file card handy to keep them clean. Have a small square to hand, then you can check if the file is running true, colour the surface with the fibre pen it will show exactly where the file is cutting. Take care cutting the tiny edge chamfers, aim to file evenly at 45° it makes the shape look crisp and sharp.

Centerpopping - see that pops are fine and sharp. Always scribe a cross to pop on, pop lightly firstly, then check you are on centre; angling the pop should correct any error. With care, it is possible to position holes to within a few thou. the loupe or magnifying glass is good for accurate inspection.

Marking out - sketch dimensions are in metric and imperial, this is to simplify accurate scribing. With a good clear rule and a sharp scriber it is possible to position a line to within a few thou. Divider points should be fine and sharp so they can be set accurately. Where possible, I prefer to produce locatable scribing guides, then, all you have to worry about is filing square. It is awkward marking small rad's with the dividers, especially if they have to be cut true to a hole.

Tapping - always check taps are sharp, a dull tap breaking can scrap hours of work. Use only good quality tapping fluid. Set level in the vice then you can look to see the tap is starting vertical. Remember, always check the front, and from the side. Have handy an inch of paraffin and an old tooth brush in an open jar, then its quick and easy to scrub cutting tools clean prior to storage, this also prevents them from rusting.

Threads - when shortening screws, see the new end is square, always de burr by filing or grinding square to the thread form, this will ensure that they start easily. Remove machining marks from screw heads with a strip of fine emery folded over a flat file. Check screwdriver tips are square parallel and sharp, damaged screw heads can ruin the appearance of almost anything.

STARTING THE MAINFRAME

The mainframes plate is cut from 8mm. thick bright drawn mild steel - a nice flat blank 50mm. x 180mm. is required - study the actual shape - all finished edges must be sharp square and de-burred (no chamfering).

See the top face is smooth and burr free - set the protractor to scribe the back face - saw/grind so as finish sharp and square on the scribe with the file - scribe the start of the bottom face (90° to the back face - it starts sharp on the bottom corner of the blank) - scribe the top face (again - square to the back face) - saw/grind so as to finish sharp and square on the top scribe with the file - study the sketch.

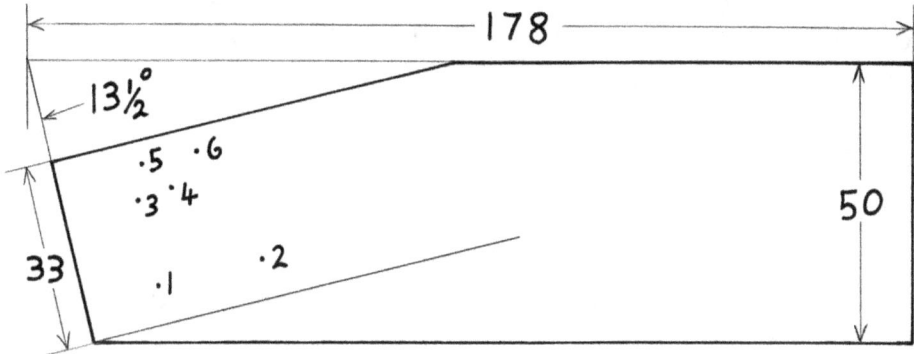

Pop the hole centres - the dim's are from the 13-1/2° edge and the bottom face scribe that is square to it (take care here - inspect closely) - study the sketch.

Hole Right Up

1 --------- 14 7 Drill hole 3 through 2mm. then 3/3/2" -
2 --------- 34 7 drill holes 1 - 2 - 4 - 5 - 6 through 2·5mm. -
3 --------- 14 23 drill hole 1 through 4mm. then 6mm. then 8mm.
4 --------- 21 24 then 11mm. - de-burr (no chamfering).
5 --------- 16 29
6 --------- 27 29 Pop the hammer pivot point - Right 41 -- Up 28

Set the dividers to scribe the 10mm. hammer clearance rad. - scribe the short face that is square to the 13-1/2° edge - scribe the barrel centerline (it is 7·5mm. below the hammers pivot point - it is parallel with the blanks top face) - scribe the loading tap recess (it is 12·5mm. below the barrel centerline - use the edge of a 2p coin to blend the recess to the barrel centerline) - scribe the 20mm. rad. that blends the short face to the tap recess - study the sketch.

Saw/chaindrill (split the waste out with a sharp little chisel) - grind close so as to finish sharp and square on the scribes with the file - study the sketch.

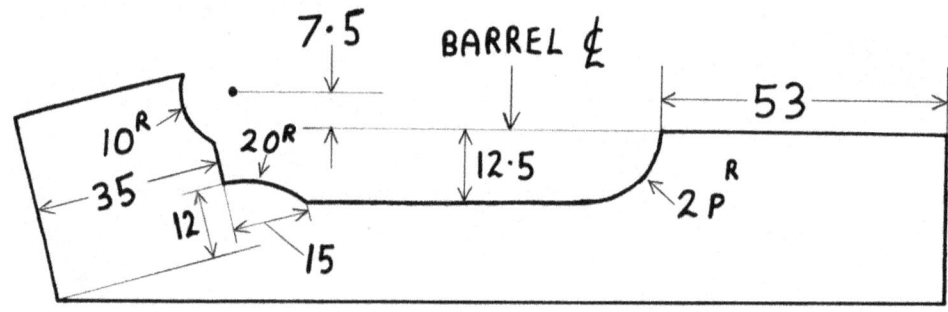

Scribe the reservoir centerline (square to the 13-1/2° face) - study the sketch - pop the firing pin hole (central to the width) - drill through with a nice sharp 2·5mm. drill (this is only the pilot hole - it is opened out and reamed at later stage) - set in the vice or clamped to the angle plate - use the square to set the centerline vertical - use a sharp drill and the cutting fluid - go steadily - so as to avoid running off.

Scribe the bottom face (parallel to the barrel centerline) - scribe the trigger and guard recess (the three edges are all square to the 13-1/2° face - use the edge of a 2p coin for the run-out rad.) - study the sketch - saw/grind so as to finish sharp and square on the scribes with the file - form the ·050 "cock stop" rad. on the featheredge (gauge this with the 2·5mm. drill shank) - study the sketch - remember - all finished edges to be sharp yet free of burring.

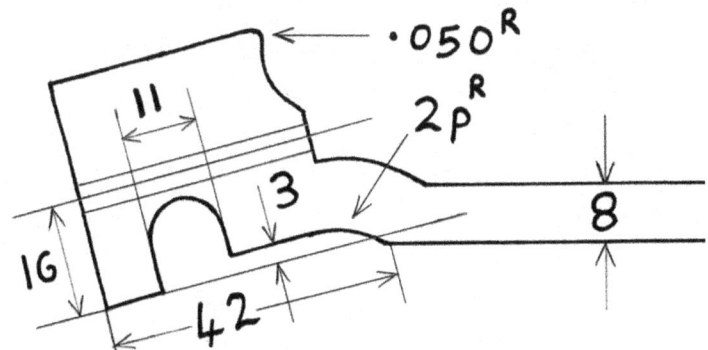

FITTING THE SOCKET

Produce the two lugs from 8mm. thick bright drawn mild steel plate (pop a piece of 8mm. plate 4mm. away from a straight edge - set the piece to be scribed alongside - set the dividers to scribe the 17mm. rad.) - saw/grind/file to shape - study the sketch.

Grind the 3 x 45° weld prep. chamfers on the lugs and on the mainframes back face so as they form a 6mm. wide vee - study the sketch (see all faces and edges are thoroughly de-burred).

To the welding bench -

The lugs must be set central to the firing pins pilot hole - they should also be square to - level with - and - butted up to - the mainframes 13-1/2° face.

Set an angle-iron off cut in the vice - use the grips to clamp the mainframe and lug to it - so as the joint is set square - eye across to see the 13-1/2° face is set level with the lug face - check the pieces are butted up tight - concentrate on getting a strong airtight weld (the joints are not visible - it is not essential that they are totally filled).

Remove slag splatter and any high weld that may hinder the setting of the other lug.

Use the warding file to remove any splatter or high weld from the lug faces - remove any weld that may have flowed over the edge of the pilot hole (chisel or die grinder).

The idea is - the firing pin slides in a non-ferrous bush - the blast flows round the firing pin and up the 5mm. hole - it then flows sideways into a slot that is milled in the left sideplate - it then flows into a hole that angles up to the loading tap.

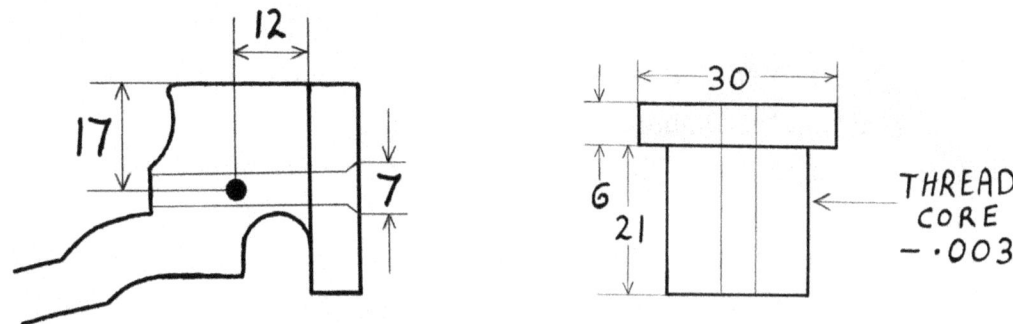

Finish the firing pin hole (set to drill as before) - start the hole off with a small centerdrill so as to form a 7mm. wide countersink that is true to the pilot hole - drill through 3·5mm. then 4·7mm. then ream through 5mm. - study the sketch.

Use the scalpel point to scrape a tiny chamfer on the front end of the reamed hole.

Pop the airway --------- from lug face --- 12 from top face --- 17 drill 4mm. x 4mm. deep - de-burr (do not chamfer) - study the sketch.

To the lathe -

Produce a "washer" type guide for scribing the weld prep. chamfer - the O.D. should be 26mm. - the hole should be reamed 5mm. - it should be concentric and de-burred (use a 2p coin).

Produce a faced and de-burred brass peg 5mm. dia. x 50mm. long.

Produce the bush for centralising the socket (aluminium or brass) - it should have a 5mm. reamed hole through the center - it should be concentric and de-burred - study the sketch.

Fit the brass peg in the airway - align the guide - scribe round - grind the 45° weld prep. chamfer running from the scribe - align the socket - it should be square to the lug face and the weld prep. chamfers should be inline (if all is not well adjust the lug face with the file).

Lock the assembly in the vice so as to weld the underside quarter (set slightly angled so as the front jaws top edge is pressing the socket against the lug face - ensure the parts have nipped together squarely - see the sockets reference pop is set so as the valves drive peg hole will align behind the trigger guard).

It is important that this joint is totally filled so it will clean up flush with the sockets O.D. (ensure the current is set correctly - avoid undercut - keep the rod tip close - avoid burning the lug edges away).

Re-set gripping on the underside of the jaws so as to weld the top quarter (again - see the faces are nipped together - combating any weld contraction pull) - remove the bush (if all is well - it should just drop out) - grip the socket lightly so as to weld the side quarters - clean - inspect closely - re-weld any low areas.

Remove splatter from the mainframe sides and lug faces (the heat from the welding may have caused the thread to contract - coat with cutting fluid then bottom the plug tap - if need be - scrub out with a paraffin soaked toothbrush).

File the lugs/weld down so as they blend flush with the socket (lock the tap in - so as to do this in the lathe?) the circular form can over-run into the plates top square edge by not more than 1mm. - study the sketch (take care here).

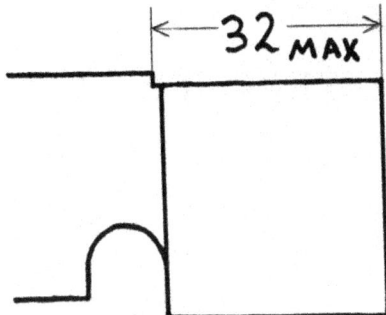

The sideplates and spacers are produced next - they are locked in position - then there square edges are shaped with the file so as they flow or blend to the lugs outer radius (the lug edges should be crisp and sharp so as the sideplates will bed up tightly - inspect closely - study the cover photograph).

THE SPRING SIDE SIDEPLATE

The spring side sideplate is made from 1/8" or 3mm. thick ground flat stock - this is also known as gauge plate or O1 steel - it can be heat treated to make it hard like a drill bit or wood chisel - it's the kind of steel that press tools and shear blades are made from - and as the name implies it comes ready surface ground in exact metric or imperial sizes - it is available from all good engineers merchants.

Produce the oversize de-burred blank - study the sketch - the bottom face should align to the datum scribe (3mm. below the trigger guard recess) - the left side should bed to the lug (it should be close to 90° depending on how accurately the lug was set) - again all finished edges should be sharp square and free of burring.

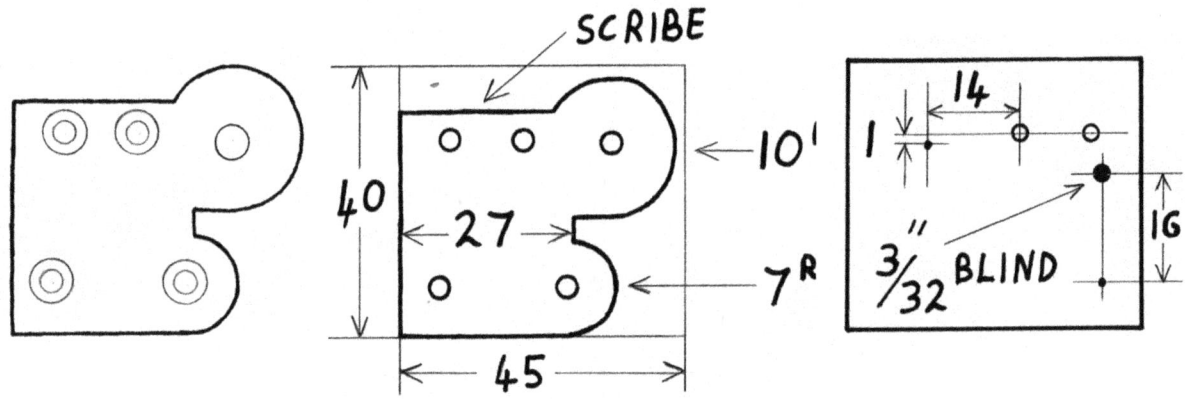

Clamp in position (grips) - mount on parallels so as to spot holes 2 5 6 (2·5mm.).

Spot hole 3 (3/32") - whilst clamped in position scribe the top face inline with the mainframe - study the sketch.

Separate - drill hole 3 about 2·5mm. deep (3/32") - de-burr - study the sketch.

Pop the trigger and hammers pivot points (for greater accuracy measure these from the spotted centers - rather than the lug edge and bottom face).

Drill both holes through 2·5mm. - de-burr - study the sketch.

Drill holes 2 5 6 through 2·5mm. - de-burr - study the sketch.

Produce two "washer" type guides for scribing the rad's true to the holes - both should have 2·5 holes - they should be de-burred and concentric - study the sketch (a 1p coin is ideal for the larger rad.).

Use the drill shank to centralise the guides (again - scribe on the underside) - saw/grind so as to finish sharp and square on the scribes with the file (use the needle files to form the detail between the rad's. - leave all edges sharp yet free of any burring) - study the sketch.

Produce five M.4 countersunk head - slot drive - machine screws - four should be 21mm. total length - one should be 15mm. total length - turn all the heads down to ·235 dia. - de-burr (the shorter screw is for securing the other sideplate - it will be required soon).

Drill holes 2 5 6 through 4mm. - sharpen a 6mm. drill so it has a 45° cutting angle (gauge with the square) - countersink the 4mm. holes so as the screws will lock in leaving the heads being about 10 thou. above the plates face - study the sketch (take care here - the sideplate relies on the countersinks for its location).

The trigger and hammer pivot holes are finished later (store the 14mm. dia. scribing guide safely - it will be required again).

THE LEFT SIDEPLATE

The left sideplate is made from 5/16" - or - 8mm. thick ground flat stock - produce the de-burred blank - study the sketch - the top face should align to the mainframes top face - the left side should bed to the lug (again - all finished edges should be sharp square and free of any burring).

Clamp in position (grips) mount on parallels so as to spot holes 2 4 5 6 (2·5mm.) - whilst clamped together scribe the sideplate inline with the loading tap recess - study the sketch.

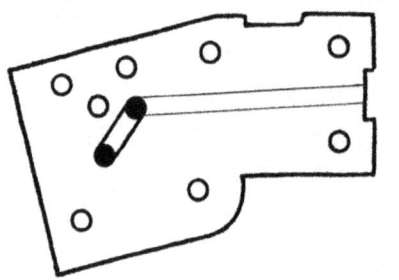 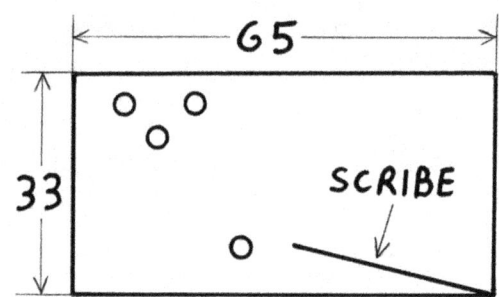

Separate - drill all holes through 2·5mm. then 3·3mm. then tap M.4 (take care - set level - tap square) - de-burr.

Lock the sideplates together with three of the prepared screws (the top and bottom faces should be inline - the end faces should be closely inline - depending on how accurately the lugs were set).

Mount on parallels so as to drill the hammer and trigger pivot holes through 2·5mm. then 3·3mm.

Drill the hammer pivot hole through 4·5mm. then ream 3/16" - separate - de-burr.

At this point - drill the spring side sideplates pivot hole out to 4mm. then countersink (the same as the other three).

Tap the trigger pivot hole M.4 - de-burr.

Set the protractor to 13-1/2° so as to scribe the front face - it is 27·5mm. forward of the hammers pivot hole centerline - study the sketch - saw/grind so as to finish sharp and square on the scribe with the file.

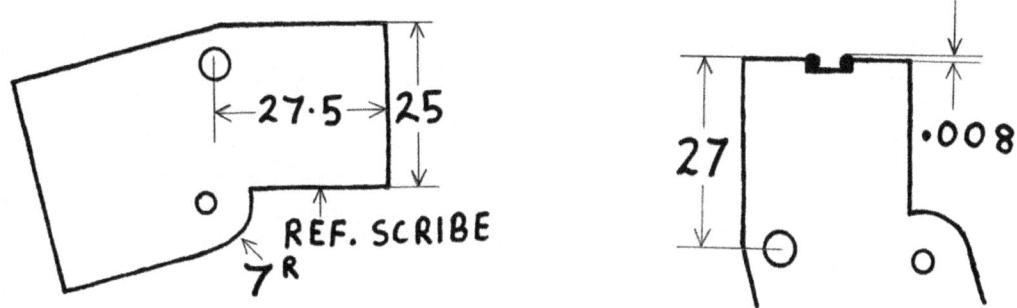

Scribe the top face - it is square to the front face - it is 25mm. above the reference scribe - saw/grind so as to finish sharp and square on the scribe with the file - study the sketch.

Drill the 14mm. dia. scribing guide out to 3·3 - scribe rad. that blends to the reference scribe - saw/grind so as to finish sharp and square on the scribes with the file - study the sketch.

Pop the "slot end" holes - 12 from edge -- 17 from top face -------------- 19 from edge -- 11 from top face - drill 4mm. x 6mm. deep - link the holes with a 1/8" milled slot 5mm. deep - de-burr - do not chamfer - study the actual shape.

Pop the airway in the centre of the front face (scribe its course - grip in the vice - use the square to set the course scribe vertical) - drill 1/8" (use a sharp drill and the cutting fluid) - de-burr - study the actual shape.

Select an O ring that is near to 8mm. O.D. x 4mm. I.D.

Set the sideplate in the milling machine vice - so as the front face is square to the spindle - set the spindle central to the faces length - zero the index.

Arm the spindle with an 8mm. cutter - skim 20 thou. off the entire face - return to the zero - index down to form the O ring recess (it should leave about 8 thou. protruding - use a good sharp cutter and a steady feed - so as the surface finishes will be nice and smooth) - study the sketch.
De-burr with the needle file - leave all edges crisp and sharp - the holes for the loading tap rivets are formed when the barrel is fitted - the recess for the rear sight is cut soon.

THE REAR SIGHT

Many of the old butt reservoir airguns had no sights whatsoever - some had only a front bead like on a shotgun - so I thought the sights for my airgun should be simple and as small as possible.

The rear sight is made from 1/16" thick (or close to) mild steel (this will cold bend without cracking and blue with the flame).

Produce a de-burred blank about 9mm. wide and about 20mm. long - one end should be nice and square - pop the fixing hole - drill and countersink for an M.3 screw (this should run out at about 4·5mm. on the face) - study the sketch.

Scribe the bend line just clear of the countersinks edge - lock in the vice so as to form a sharp 90° bend (use the hammer) - study the sketch.

Drill/tap the sideplate (set the depth stop) - study the sketch (thin the cutting oil with paraffin then remove the swarf with a magnet attached to a wire) - lock the blank in precise position with a suitably prepared screw - scribe the recess edges.

Set the sideplate in the milling machine vice - so as to cut the recess - touch on with small sharp cornered cutter - index down to the thickness of the stock - work to the rear scribe - work to the front scribe with a cutter that will leave a suitable corner rad. so as the sight will lock in and bed flush - de-burr - study the sketch.

Lock the sight in position - saw the waste off so as to leave the blade being about 2·5mm. high - file the sides off so as they are flush with the sideplate - use the square needle file to cut the vee - it should be about 1mm. deep - it should be symmetrical and central (the top face and vee should angle down slightly - so as the backside will appear crisp and sharp - take care here) - remove - de-burr thoroughly - store safely.

THE SPACERS

The spacers fit between the spring side sideplate and the mainframe - the top and front spacers are cut from 1/8" thick ground flat stock (the trigger mechanism is cut from 3mm. thick ground flat stock - the spacers allow an exact clearance so as the moving parts can operate freely and precisely).

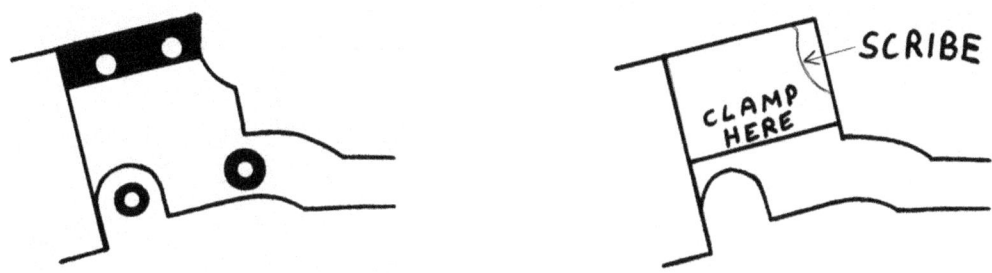

Front spacer - pop the stock so as to scribe a 10mm. circle (dividers) - drill through 2·5mm. then 4mm. - saw out - de-burr.

Face then drill/tap a 1/4" bar end M.4 - lock the blank on - so as to turn the O.D. to ·312 and be true to the hole (leave edges sharp - yet free of any burring).

The top spacer doubles as the mechanisms dust cover - produce a burr-free over-size blank - clamp in position (with the grips - below the holes) - study the sketch - the top faces should be inline - the back face should be bedded to the lug.

Mount on narrow parallels so as to spot the two holes (2·5) - whilst clamped together scribe the front rad's. inline with the mainframes rad's. - remove - drill the holes through then open out for the screws (these should be minimal clearance so as to prevent the spacer from floating about - try 3·9) - de-burr.

Scribe the bottom face (it is only 20 thou. below the edge of the holes - study the actual shape) - saw/grind - so as to finish sharp and square on the scribes with the file - de-burr thoroughly.

The back spacer is also the triggers pivot point - it is made from 6mm. dia. silversteel (this is basically the same as ground flat stock - but in bar form - it too comes in exact metric or imperial sizes - with a nice ground finish).

This spacer should have a minimal clearance hole for the 4mm. screw - it should be concentric - with ends faced square - and de-burred - its length should be the thickness of the mainframe plate plus ·125 exactly - inspect with the micrometer.

SHAPING

Now for the shaping work - drill holes 2 4 5 6 through 4mm. - countersink hole 4 for the shorter screw made earlier (the head should lock in and be a few thou. lower than the plates face) - de-burr - study the sketch.

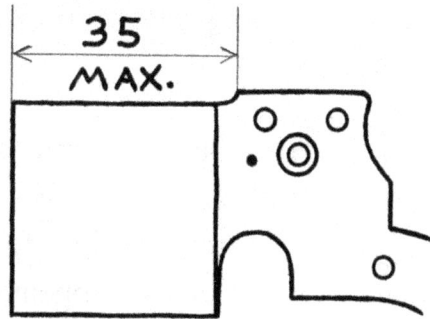

Use the 1/4" dia. chainsaw file to blend the plate down to the socket (the internal radius should run out leaving a sharp and square edge that runs across the plates top face - take care here - avoid over-filing) - study the sketch.

Lock the left sideplate in position with the hole 4 screw (the top faces should be flush and the other screw holes should be perfectly inline).

The idea is - the sockets radial profile should flow out and blend to a sharp square edge that runs across the actions top face - now remove the sideplates sharp corner with the chainsaw file (start the file off at an angle - on the very corner - guide the file against your thumb end - so as to get a start) - then work roundward and sideward so as to form a nice internal rad. that blends the mainframe plates rad. down to the socket - aim at leaving the top corner square and sharp (take care here - study the cover photograph).

Lock the spring side sideplate and spacers in position (if all is well all the parts should fit together perfectly - all the top faces should be flush - the plate ends should be tight up to the lugs and the screw ends should all be about 1mm. below the sideplate face).

Use the same technique so as to blend the sideplate and spacer to the sockets radial profile - study the cover photograph.

Round off both sideplates bottom edges (this is also a continuation of the sockets profile - the rad's. should be parallel to the plates edges and they should run out close to the M.4 threads and countersinks) - rough down on the grinder - finish with the file - study the cover photograph.

At this point - the sockets finish should be part filed and part turned - when all is well in the shaping department run the needle file all over the sockets O.D. so as the finish is even (I would say that the needle filed finish is right for this type of action - to go beyond could ruin the hand-made - or old looking appearance).

Scribe down the edge of the sideplates so as to put a good sharp line on the lug faces - dismantle - remove all burring from all parts - leave all edges crisp and sharp.

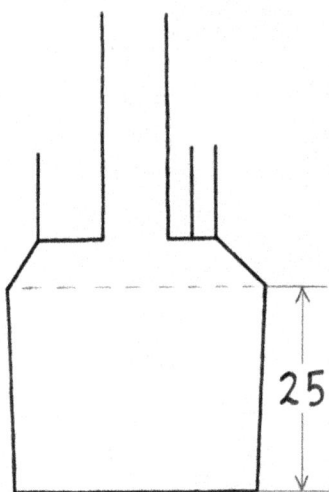

File the blending angles on the lugs (scribe the socket sides - grip the socket set angled - so as to file on the level - look for the flat merging with both scribes) - study the sketch - assemble for inspection - if all is well strip down and store the parts safely.

Pop the securing holes for the mainspring and its stop - drill through 3mm. then 5·5mm. then tap 1/4" U.N.F. - de-burr - form the full rad. on the front end (use the edge of a 1p coin to guide the scriber) - de-burr - study the sketch.

THE TRIGGER GUARD

Set the mainframe in the vice so as to drill/tap the M.4 fixing hole (set the depth stop) - study the sketch - the guard is made from 1/16" x 5/8" or 1·5mm. x 15mm. ground flat stock - a 106mm. long blank is required - study the actual shape.

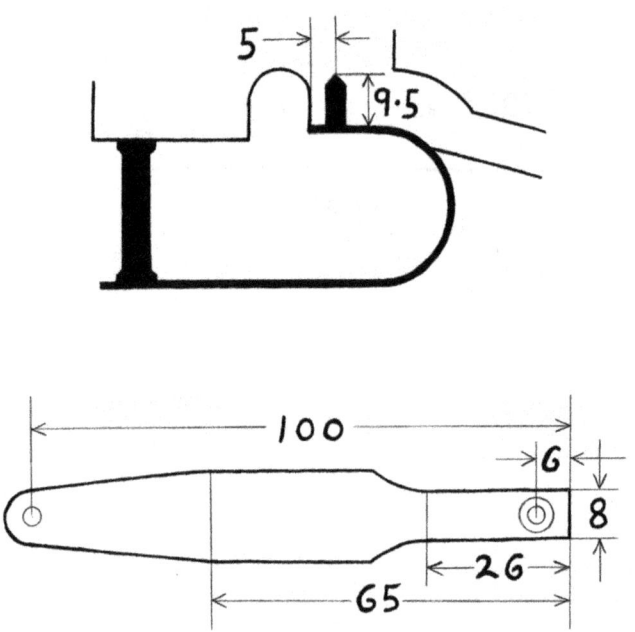

Polish the face with fine emery so the scribes will appear crisp and clear - file a square end - scribe the internal rad. centerline - scribe the front parallel edges.

Form the internal rad's. (sink the half round file down on the centerline) - saw the waste off - file to the parallel scribes - de-burr - study the sketch.

Pop the fixing holes - drill through 2·5mm. then 4mm. - countersink at 45° - (they should run out at about 6mm. dia. on the face - this should allow for forming a slight dome on the screw heads - take care here - they are on opposite sides) - de-burr - study the sketches.

Scribe the 5mm. rad. true to the hole (turn a "rivet" type guide) - scribe the angles - grind/file to shape - form a full rad. on the edges (running from the internal rad. run out - to - the internal rad. run out) - so the guard will not be sharp to the touch.

Bending the guard (this is what I did) - produce a steel roller 23mm. dia. about 3/4" long (ends faced square) - set in the edge of the vice jaws to start the bend off - the point of grip is about 14mm. from the end of the strip - study the sketch.

(Mark the edge with the fibre pen - set looking into the countersink) - grip lightly - tap the roller so it is vertical - tap the strip so it is horizontal then lock in position - bend the strip round until it hits the jaw - study the sketch.

Align for inspection (the end of the guard should be about 1mm. past the recess edge - the bend should bed in the mainframes radius - the screw holes should be inline - and it should look fairly square).

Re-set so as to bend the strip further round - study the sketch.

Set with a narrow spacer block forward of the roller - so as to finish the bend - study the sketch - lock up tight - use a small hammer with a smooth crown face to tap the strip to the roller - aim at forming the perfect letter U with a 24mm. internal diameter.

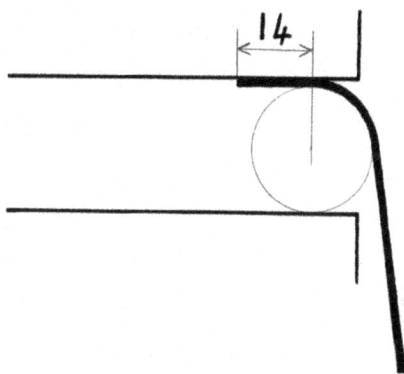

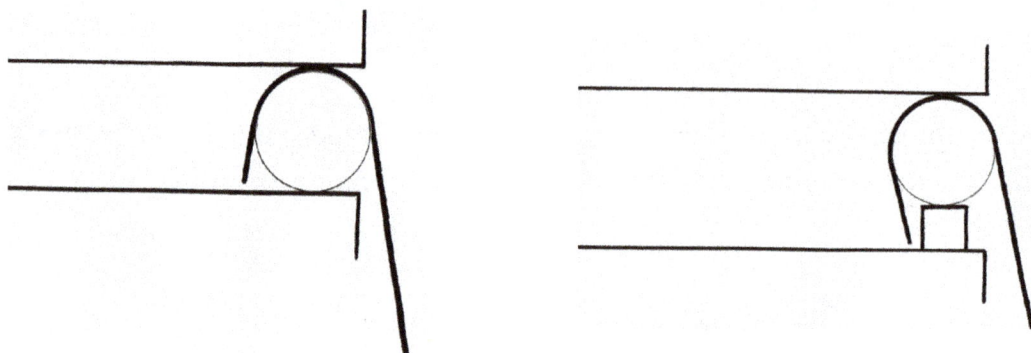

Produce the spacer bar (8mm. dia. mild steel) - set an over-long blank in the 3 jaw - drill 3·3mm. x 27mm. deep - set against the revolving center so as to form the relief with a round pointed tool - the middle section should be about 6mm. dia. - the bars finished length should be 24mm. - the relief should run out so as to leave about 1·5mm. of the 8mm. dia. at each end - study the cover photograph.

Set in the vice so as to tap M.4 x 12mm. deep then part to length.

Produce two countersunk head slot drive machine screws of suitable length - set in the lathe to form a slight dome on the heads (file - needle file - fine emery).

Hold the guard in precise position (the end gap should be close to 24mm.) - mark the screwdriver hole - it must be directly inline with the fixing screws course - set in the vice to drill out in stages to 6mm. - de-burr.

Lock the guard in position - fine tune so as the end gap is exactly 23·5mm. - fit the spacer bar - if all is well it should look central and square - it should also be under very slight tension (so as the guard is clamping it to the socket - perfect for silver soldering the joint).

Check the assembly is set inline with the mainframe plate - if all is well heat so as to run a nice even ring of silver solder round the joint (see silver and lead soldering) - let cool - clean - tidy with the round needle file - if need be.

File the end of the guard off so as to leave a sharp 90° corner on the trigger recess edge (be certain the guards side faces do not protrude beyond the edges of the mainframe in the recess area - inspect closely) - remove - de-burr - store safely.

Store the "rivet" type guide safely - it will be required later.

BITS AND BOBS

Produce the firing pin bush (phosphor bronze is best - but hard brass is fine) - it should be 14·5mm. long with faced ends - it should have a 1/8" reamed hole through the center - it should be a nice slide fit in the 5mm. hole - it should be concentric and de-burred.

Set the bush so as 1·5mm. protrudes - heat so as to run a nice even ring of silver solder round the end - let cool - re-ream (by hand - grip the reamer in a small chuck) - fit the reservoir (bottom the plug tap again - if need be - then wash/scrub out with a paraffin soaked toothbrush).

The firing pin is made from 1/8" silversteel - it should be a nice slide fit in the bush - set in the lathe to face (leave the edge sharp - yet de-burred) - fit the reservoir - set the pin in position so as the faced end is touching on the valve head - use the fiber pen to mark the length (the tip should be faced and slightly domed with the needle file - it should protrude by 5mm.).

Fit the pin in position so as to mark it inline with the 4mm. airway hole (fiber pen) - remove the reservoir - pull the pin out (from the back) - place in the vee block so as to position a centerpop on the mark (the bruise prevents the pin from sliding forward - the pop is fairly central "so" should the pin ever slide out - "remember" ---------- the sharp square end hits valve).

Produce the hammers pivot pin from 5mm. silversteel - turn the ·187 - inspect with the sideplates reamed hole - form the full rad. with the file - smooth with the needle file and fine emery - turn the other ·187 so as it leaves the 11mm. wide shoulder - inspect as before - face to length - study the sketch.

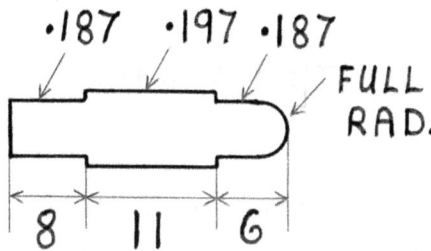

Now lock the left sideplate in position with the hole 4 screw.

THE HAMMER

The hammer is cut from ground flat stock - it should be exactly the same width as the mainframe - bright drawn mild steel is usually a few thou. undersize - the 8mm. or ·315 may actually be closer to 5/16" or ·312 - inspect before obtaining stock - a 70mm. x 30mm. blank is required - see the left edge is smooth and burr free - see the face is smooth and clean so the scribes will appear crisp and sharp - study the actual shape.

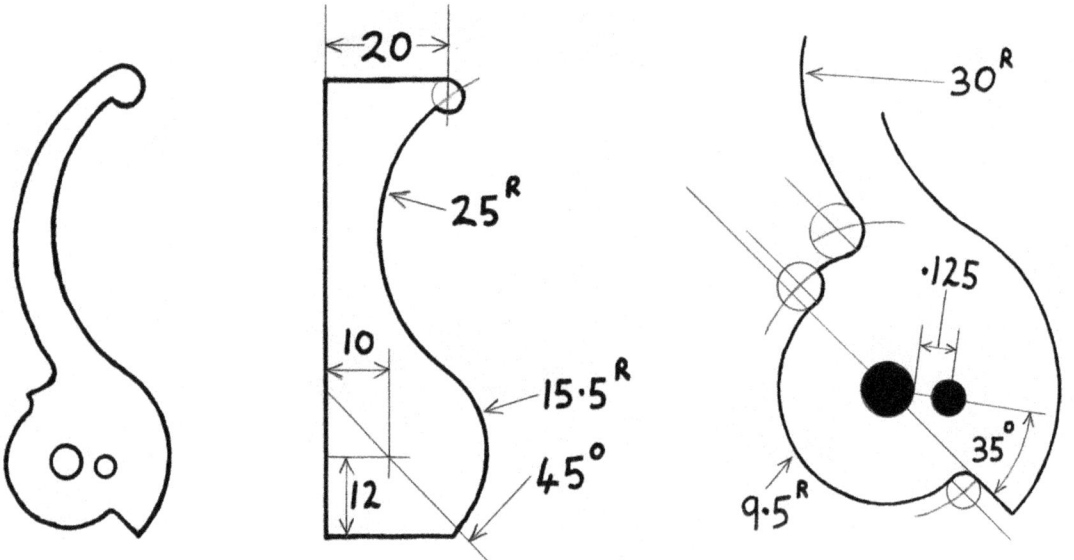

Pop the pivot hole (scribe only a small cross to pop on) - set the dividers to scribe the 15·5mm. rad. - scribe the 5mm. ball (use the divider points to hold a suitable washer on the edge of the blank then scribe round the hole) - study the sketch.

Set the dividers to scribe the 25mm. rad. - it clips the 15·5mm. rad. - it runs through the center of the ball - scribe straight lines to hacksaw to - chaindrill - split the waste off with a sharp little chisel - grind close - finish sharp and square on the scribes with the file - study the sketch.

Set the protractor to scribe the hammer faceline (45°) - it runs through the center of the pop - drill three holes that help form the shape (set the dividers to scribe the rad's from the pivot pop - measure square from the faceline) - study the sketch.

Pop the 3mm. hole that forms the top of the hammers faceline - 11rad. --- left 1·5

pop the 4mm. hole that forms the "cock stop" - 11·5rad. --- right 1

pop the 5mm. hole that forms the bottom of the arm - 14rad. --- right 6·5

drill through - de-burr - do not chamfer - study the sketch.

Set the dividers to scribe the 9·5mm. rad. - this clips the edges of the 3&4mm. holes - set the protractor to scribe the centerline for the mainspring links pivot pin - it runs through the center of the pivot hole pop - study the sketch.

Drill the pivot hole through 3mm. then 4·7mm. then ream 5mm. - de-burr.

Pop the hole for the mainspring links pivot pin - the center should be ·125 away from the edge of the pivot hole (fit a 5mm. drill shank or dowel in the hole - measure from the edge) - drill through 2·5mm. then 2·9mm. then ream 1/8" - de-burr - study the sketch.

Set the dividers to scribe the 30mm. rad. - it clips the edge of the 5mm. hole - it clips the edge of the ball - saw/chaindrill - grind close - so as to finish sharp and square on the scribes with the file - study the actual shape.

Remove any scribe marks with fine emery - use the needle file to cut a tiny chamfer all round the edges (on both sides).

Produce the links pivot pin (1/8" silversteel) - the ends should be faced and de-burred - the length should be the thickness of the mainframe plus ·120 exactly - inspect with the micrometer.

Assemble all the parts - lock the spring side sideplate in position - be certain that the pivot pins shoulders clear the sideplates (if all is well the sideplate should lock down flat on all of the spacers and the hammer should flop back and forth freely) - if all is not well - make adjustments now.

THE MAINSPRING LINK

The link allows the mainspring to transmit all its power to the hammer so it can rotate with maximum acceleration.

Produce two "rivet" type scribing guides for marking the link - (stalk ·125 --- head ·250) --- (stalk ·250 --- head ·590).

The link is cut from 5mm. thick ground flat stock - a 16mm. x 35mm. blank is required - see the face is clean so the scribes will appear crisp and sharp.

Scribe the centerlines - pop the hole centers - drill the pivot pin hole 2·5mm. then 2·9mm. then ream 1/8" - de-burr - drill the socket 2·5mm. then 4mm. then 6mm. then ream 1/4" - de-burr.

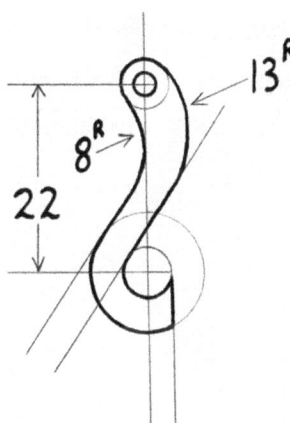

Use the guides to scribe the 1/8" and 7·5mm. rad's - scribe the 8mm. rad. (use the edge of a suitable washer) - it clips the 1/8" rad. - it clips the centerline - it then blends to a straight scribe that angles to the 7·5mm. rad. - study the sketch.

Scribe down from the edge of the socket - this short scribe runs parallel with the centerline - scribe the angle running from the socket - it is parallel with the other angled scribe - blend the angle to the 1/8" rad. with a 13mm. rad. (use a 2p coin).

Saw/grind close - finish the 1/8" rad. first - it should clear the hammers pivot pin by just a few thou. - assemble to inspect when you near the scribe - form the "hook" end then remove the sharp featheredge.

Take care filing the lower angle - see it blends in square to the sockets reamed finish - feather the end of the 7·5mm. rad. down slightly - study the actual shape (aim at creating the "crane hook shape" - delicate yet strong).

Thin the top down so it fits under the sideplate (set on a flat surface - use a piece of 3mm. plate to guide the scriber) - the ·118 section should run out in a radius - this should merge roughly inline with the middle of the socket hole (allow for this when sawing) - study the cover photograph.

File the ·118 section - inspect with the micrometer when you near the scribe - form the run out rad. with the half round file - when all is well - cut a tiny chamfer all round the edges with the needle file - assemble for inspection - store the smaller scribing guide safely - it will be required later.

THE TRIGGER MECHANISM

For any rifle to shoot well a smooth trigger release system is essential - A stiff or unsmooth trigger will impair the aiming of any rifle - On this type of gun the hammer must deliver quite a powerful blow - compared against most powder powered weapons - Hence - copying a "standard" hammer release system would not (I think) suffice - For example - if you were to cock a normal type hammer gun then forcefully push the hammer foreword the trigger would require a much stronger pull to cause its release - If you beef up the power of the spring - you have also got to beef up the size of the release mechanism so as the leverage points will not be overloaded - This mechanism must be small - smooth - reliable and above all - safe - When you study the picture on the cover you may think that the mechanism behind the sideplate would be crude and simple - I experimented with many crude and simple ideas - but none would work - Sorting out an initial route towards a suitable design took me ages - then it took me more ages to find the end of the route - If you think design is easy - Read no more - Close the book - Study the cover picture - Then go and design a suitable trigger mechanism ----

O.K. first you want to have a quick look at what I did.

Here is a "Jesus like" parable that should explain the mechanical principal and give you a clue – An old man was sheltering underneath a massive water tank - it was supported upon four large corner columns - He was standing on a nice flat concrete floor - the tanks base was 10 feet above the concrete - Suddenly the tank started to fill - as the fill increased he noticed that the bottom had started to bulge - Ideally he needed a good stout wooden beam that was ten feet long to jamb underneath - He searched desperately - there was no ten foot beam - All he could find was a long weedy stick and two short beams - One beam was five feet long - the other was five feet and a quarter of an inch - He raced back and jammed the two beams under the tank - they would not fit exactly inline - so he had to stand there and support them -

The tank filled more - he could tell there was immense downward pressure on the beams - yet the sidereal pressure seemed small - Holding the beams was "easy work" he could read the paper and have a fag - but he couldn't walk away - Down the road came a pretty girl - she smiled at the old man - then she said will you take me to the pictures - He could have released his supporting hold smoothly and safely - and then moved out of the way - But that would have triggered off the tanks destruction - The girl was very pretty - He studied the situation - Then - the penny dropped - he got the girl to position the long weedy stick so as it jammed the beams in position - then the clever old bugger shot off to the pictures ------ with the pretty girl.

Producing the trigger mechanism ---- guided by the parable.

The first job is to drill and ream a 1/8" hole in the hammer - this is for the drag bars pivot pin (the drag bar is one of the old mans short beams) - set the hammer faceline touching on the firing pin bush - scribe a line running from the center of the hammers pivot pin - to - the center of hole 6 - study the sketch.

The drag bars pivot pin is on this line - and - the center should be ·125 away from the edge of the hammers pivot hole (measure from a drill shank/dowel as before) - pop - inspect - drill through 2·5mm. then 2·9mm. then ream 1/8" - de-burr.

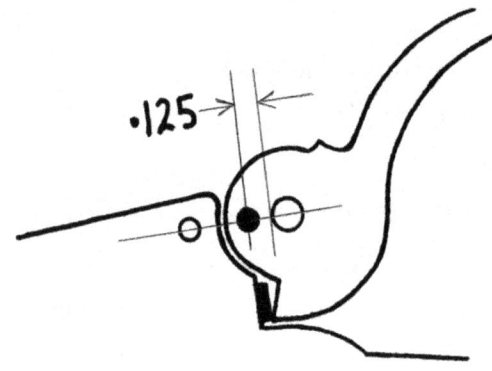

Produce the pivot pin (1/8" silversteel) - the ends should be faced and de-burred - the length should be the thickness of the mainframe plus ·120 exactly - inspect with the micrometer.

This is how it works - study the sketch - the hammer cocks - as it rotates the drag bar pushes the center bar backwards - and then it starts to pull it forwards - the hammer hits the cock stop - at this point the drag bar will have pulled the center bar slightly further forward than it was in the first place - this allows the spring loaded trigger plate to turn and lock them in position (like the weedy stick) - at this point the three pivot points should be closely inline (like the old mans beams under the tank) - the points should not be able to reach "dead inline" this would cause the hammer to be jammed back - but - they must be close so as to minimise the sidereal pressure (hence - a nice smooth trigger release).

It is most important that the hammer and trigger mechanism operate freely - so as to ensure consistency in the firing cycle - no moving part should be rubbing jamming or binding - all edges should be burr free and the moving parts should all have clearance - otherwise will lead to trouble and make manufacture difficult.

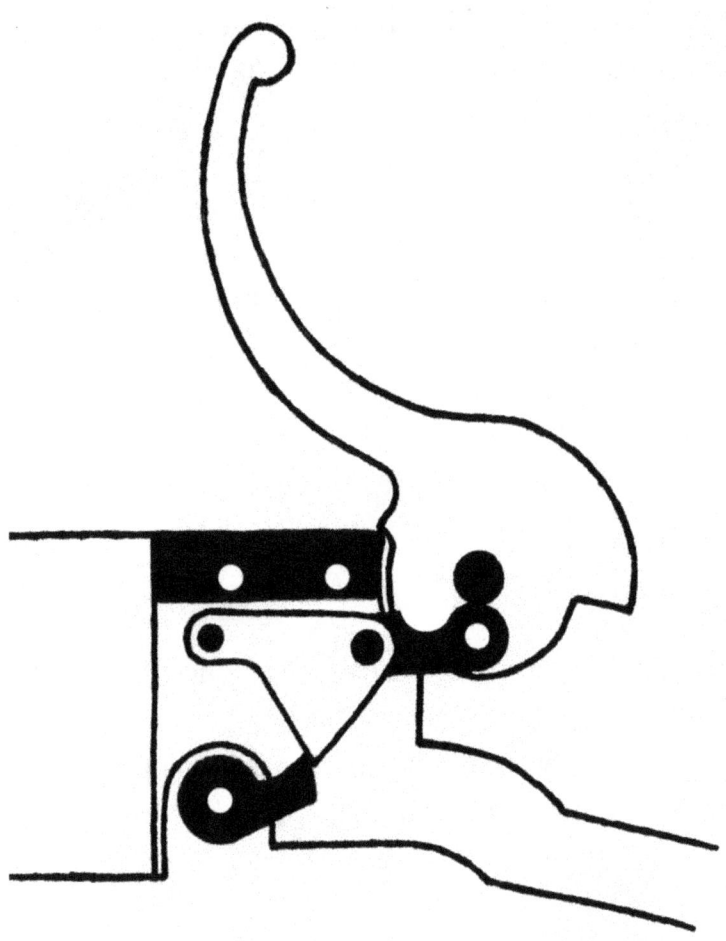

Produce the center bars pivot pin (3/32" silversteel - or an old drill shank) - it should have square and de-burred ends - it should be about 13mm. long (check the length - be certain the sideplate will bed flat on all of the spacers).

Starting the center bar (3mm. ground flat stock) - study the sketch - scribe the centerlines 4mm. in from a square edge - pop the pivot hole - set the dividers to scribe the 16mm. rad. - pop the drag bars pivot point - study the sketch.

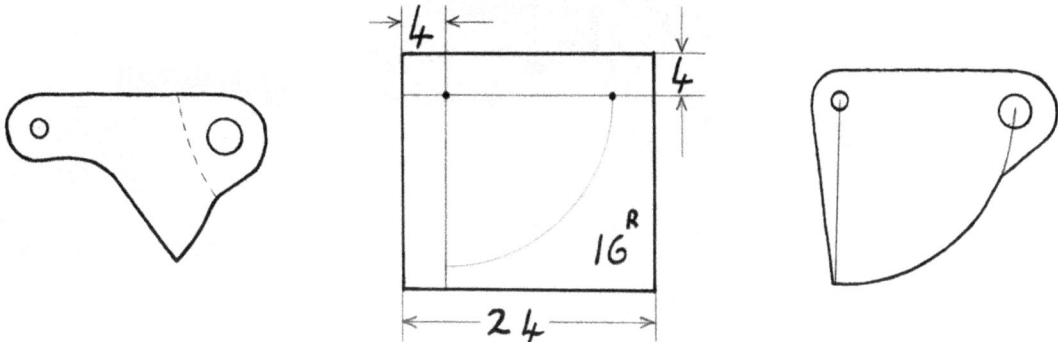

Drill the pivot hole through 2·2mm. then ream 3/32" - de-burr - drill the drag bars pivot point through 2·5mm. then 2·9mm. then ream 1/8" - de-burr - study the sketch.

Produce another "rivet" type guide (stalk ·093 ---- head ·236) - use this and the guide made for the mainspring link job for marking the 1/8" & 3mm. rad's. true to the pivot holes - study the sketch.

Connect the 3mm. rad. to the centerline and 1/8" rad. - connect the 1/8" rad. to the 16mm. rad. - saw/grind so as to finish sharp and square on the scribes with the file - de-burr - study the sketch.

Fit the top spacer (with screws) - fit the bar on its pivot pin - be certain the bars 3mm. rad. clears the spacer by a few thou. (just minimal clearance here).

The drag bar is made from 1mm. thick ground flat stock - it pivots in a sawn slot - it is essential that this is cut square and central (this is what I did) - mount a ·040 slitting wheel in the lathe chuck - drill/tap the back end of an old lathe tool - so as to attach the center bar with a clamp - fit a 1/8" dowel on the front/underside (so as to prevent the bar from pulling round) - study the sketch - set the assembly locked in the toolpost (set square - and - at the right height) - zero the slide index (just over 1/16" past the holes edge) - touch on the side - pitch over ·079 - then steadily feed in to the zero (cutting oil).

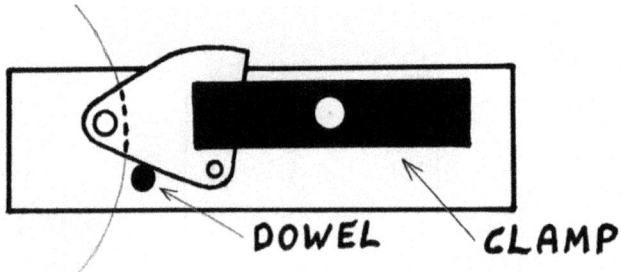

De-burr thoroughly - produce the pivot pin (1/8" silversteel) - it should be faced and de-burred and exactly ·118 long.

Now for some accurate ruler measuring - set the action lying flat - set the hammer fully back - measure the distance from the center of the 3/32" hole - to - the center of the drag bars pin hole (press the hammer against the sideplate - take care - this is the height of the water tank) - it should be "close" to 27mm. - one of our short beams is 16mm. long (the center bar) - our other short beam (the drag bar) should be made so as the combined measurement is half a mm. longer than the total - then the hammer cannot jamb back - and - the sidereal pressure will be minimal.

In simple ---- "if" ---- the total is   27
                                        minus the center bar $\underline{16}$
                                        = 11 -- so -- the drag bar should be 11·5 long.

Pop the centers - drill 2·5mm. then 2·9mm. then ream 1/8" - use the guide to scribe the rad's - saw/file to shape - de-burr - assemble (inspection is tricky - the sockets centerline should be about 1-1/2mm. out of alignment when the hammer is fully back - see the hammer is bedded to the sideplate and its pivot pin is square - take care here) - if all is well - relieve the bar so as it will clear the top spacer when the hammer is fully forward - study the sketch.

Form the flat for the trigger plate to engage on - cock the hammer slightly - so as the drag bar is pushing the center bar back to its furthest position - scribe the flat - it starts inline with the edge of the trigger relief gap - it runs inline with the front edge of the pivot holes 3mm. rad. - study the sketch (the flat should be square and smoothed with fine emery).

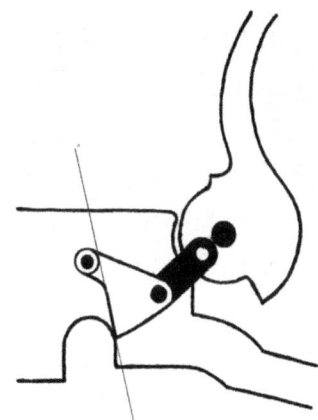

The trigger assembly pivots on the spacer - it is made in three parts that are silver soldered together - the plate (nearest) - the spacer washer - and the bit you pull on (the washer positions the pull so it is in the center of the mainframe - the return spring fits into the space that is left underneath).

Produce a scribing guide/soldering jig (mild steel) - the stalk should be ·236 dia. x 8mm. long - the head should be ·390 dia. x 8mm. long - it should be concentric and have a M.4 tapped hole through the center (for clamping the parts inline).

Lock the spacer in position (produce a screw with a small cap head) - the plate is made from 3mm. ground flat stock - set the hammer fully back - measure from the center of the spacer - to - the flat - pop the stock 5mm. in from a straight edge - scribe the centerline parallel to the edge - set the dividers to scribe the larger rad. - study the sketch.

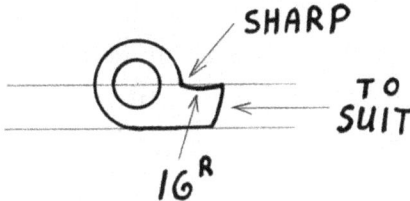

Drill the pivot hole through 2·5mm. then 4·5mm. then 5·7mm. then ream 6mm. - de-burr - use the jig to scribe the 5mm. rad. - saw/file to shape (it is most important that larger rad. is formed true and square - with a smooth finish).

Fit on the spacer for inspection - set the hammer fully forward - see the center bars flat clears the plates 5mm. rad. (the hammer should pull to full cock - the plate should be able to turn - then the hammer should push forward slightly - proving there is a small amount of clearance) - if all is well - form the 16mm. rad. that allows the plate bed to the bar - study the sketch.

The trigger pull is made from 1/8" or 3mm.thick ground flat stock - scribe the centrelines - pop the pivot hole - drill through so as to ream 6mm. - de-burr - use the guide to scribe the 5mm. rad. - set the dividers to scribe the larger rad's. so as to leave the tail 3mm. wide - saw/file to shape - de-burr - study the sketch.

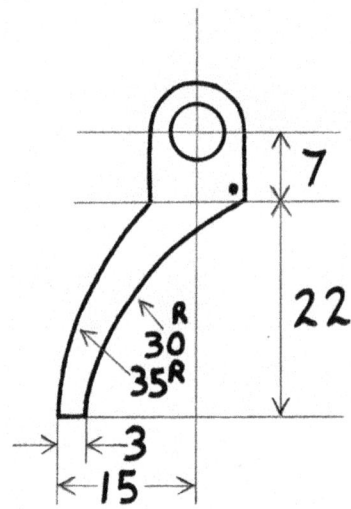

Drill the 1mm. hole for the return spring - it is 1·5mm. up from the scribe - it is 1·5mm in from the edge - study the sketch - turn over - countersink with the 3mm. drill (sink in so as the drill point is cutting at full dia. - it allows the return springs tail to fit in better) - file a full rad. on the 30mm. rad. so the pull is not sharp to the touch - file a full rad. on the 3mm. tail flat.

Produce the 2·5mm. thick spacer washer (brass) - it should be 8mm. dia. - it should have a 6mm. reamed hole through the center - it should be flat (drill/ream on the lathe - face - index - part - de-burr with the scalpel point).

Fit the pull and plate on the pivot - set the hammer fully back - hold the pull pushed fully forward and up against the plate - set the plate so it is engaged by not more than 2mm. - look square on - so as to position a "clock finger" type scribe on the parts.

Set the parts in the jig (spacer in position and clock finger scribes aligned) - clamp with a pan head screw and washer - stand on the jig head so as the joint is horizontal (capillary action should cause the solder to flow round both joints - equally and evenly - avoid over-filling - one tiny blob should be sufficient).

Clean all faces and edges thoroughly - inspect (in the case of under-engagement - file the end of the trigger guard) - (in the case of over-engagement - re-form the trigger plates 16mm. rad.).

File the back of the trigger pull (just enough - so as to allow the plate to rotate and disengage - then re-blend to the 35mm. rad.).

The return spring is made from a good quality spring steel safety pin (granny's sewing tin) - the one I used was made from ·034 wire - grip in the vice so as to pull the head off (pliers) - bend the end 3/16" sharply to 90° so as to form the tail - fit the 6mm. drill shank in the trigger assembly - fit the tail in the 1mm. hole - bend the arm round the drill shank - so as to form the shape.

Fit the assembly on the pivot pin to inspect the bend - if all is well - cut the arm to length (the end of the arm must not pull up and touch the recess side - this will result in malfunction) - take care here - trim the tail if need be.

Assemble for accurate inspection - set the sideplate on the pivot pins - slide the top spacer in - fit the two screws - slide the front spacer in - fit the screw - tighten the screws to just off nipped - pull the hammer fully back - slide the trigger assembly in (with spring attached) - fit the screw - now lock all screws.

The hammer should pull to full cock - the spring loaded plate should turn and click into position - engaging by not more than 2mm. - the hammer should move forward slightly proving clearance exists - push on the hammer so as to load the mechanism - the pull should feel smooth and even - causing release.

Be certain the trigger pulls tail does not hit the guard - assemble to inspect.

Produce two small brass washers (they fit on the drag bars pivot pin - they just keep it inline) - they should be ·250 dia. x ·039 thick - they should have a 1/8" reamed hole - they should be concentric and thoroughly de-burred (drill/ream - face with a sharp little parting tool - index over the parting tools width plus ·039) - part - de-burr - inspect with the micrometer.

THE LOADING TAP

The loading tap is designed to accept calibers up to ·250 and barrels of up to 16mm. dia. - first I will explain how I fabricated a simple smoothbore barrel in ·250 cal. - obtain a nice straight length of seamless hydraulic tubing - 1/4" bore x 3/8" O.D. - this is a standard imperial stock size - it is sometimes referred to as 3/8" O.D. x 16 s.w.g. wall - (I thought 27" or over - for appearance sake).

For the outer tube - I again used seamless hydraulic tube - 15mm. O.D. with a 12mm. bore - face the ends of the bore tube - de-burr - face the ends of the outer tube so it is 1/4" shorter than the bore tube - de-burr.

Produce three faced and de-burred spacer bushes about 1/2" long (brass) - they should be a nice slide fit on the bore tube - they should be a nice slide fit in the outer tube - and they should be concentric.

Fit one bush in the middle of the bore tube (soft lead solder) - fit the assembly into the outer tube so as 1/8" protrudes at each end - fit the end bushes so as their end faces are 1/8" deeper than the ends of the outer tube.

Heat so as to fill the wells with silver solder (the protrusion just prevents any flux flowing into the bore) - face the loading tap end - de-burr - face the front end - form a slight dish running to the bore (scraper) - round the outer edge slightly (file - needle file) - polish with fine emery and wet/dry.

The loading tap is made from 25mm. x 20mm. ground flat stock - a de-burred blank 54mm. long is required - scribe the datum line 1mm. in from the sawn edge - scribe the front shoulder run out point - pop the tap hole center - set the dividers to scribe the tap holes diameter - study the sketch.

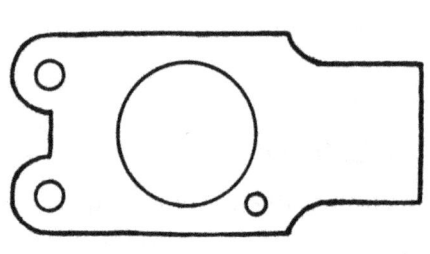 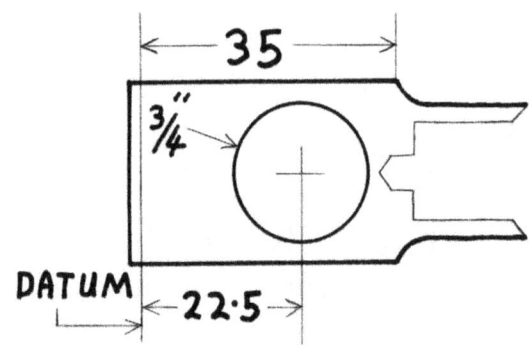

Set the blank in the 4 jaw so as the tool is clipping all four corners equally - face lightly - turn the barrel socket with a tool that will leave a 5mm. corner rad. (it should leave a wall thickness of about 2mm. around the barrel - the rad. must run out inline with the front scribe) - take care - study the sketch.

Centerdrill - drill 4·2mm. (the drill point should stop about 1/16" short of the tap hole wall scribe - take care here) - study the sketch.

Form a flat bottom counterbore - it should be a nice slide fit on the barrel - it should leave about 1/8" of the 4·2mm. hole - study the sketch - set the compound to cut the 45° chamfer for the silver solder joint (it should run out to leave a very small flat on the front face) - de-burr - study the sketch.

Re-set to face off to the datum line - remove - de-burr.

Form the tap hole (the actual dia. is not critical so long it is close to ·750) - more important is that it is cut square to the face - and that it is parallel - with a good surface finish - it can be reamed or bored - set on parallels in the drill/miller vice - or set in the 4 jaw (with the face clocked square).

De-burr then scrape a tiny chamfer on both sides with the scalpel point.

Turn the tap - it should be a nice slide fit in the hole (phosphor bronze is best but hard brass is fine) - use a tool that will leave a sharp corner in the shoulder - the end face should protrude by 5-8 thou. when the shoulder is bedded to the face - study the sketch.

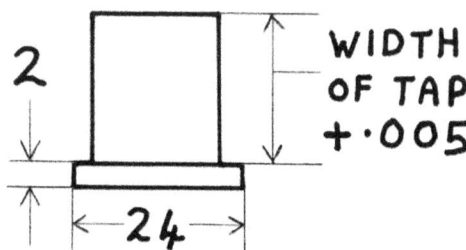

Set square in the vice so as to drill the 4·2mm. hole all the way through the assembly (fit a large washer over the protruding tap end - so as the tap shoulder will clamp hard up to the face - use a sharp drill - press lightly as you break into the tap - this should prevent pushing a steel burr into the softer material - this would cause deep scoring marks when the tap is removed).

Sink the appropriate drill or drill/reamer to suit the caliber - go only about three quarters of the way through the tap (negative rake - press lightly) - take care.

Remove from the vice (do not remove the tap) - clean out (cotton bud) - fit the reamer or drill so it secures the tap in precise position - scribe the centerline for the lever securing screws - pop - drill 3·3mm. x 17mm. deep - tap M.4 x 14mm. deep - de-burr (pop the front end of the tap - so as to prevent any confusion when re-assembling) - study the sketch.

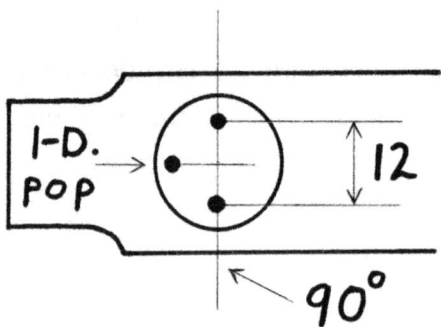

Scribe the centerline on the top face - pop the loading port hole - fold a strip of medium emery over a flat file - grip so as to hold the strip taught then ward off the protruding tap - so as the face is nice and flat - dismantle - clean thoroughly.

Set the tap in the drill vice so as to finish cutting the bore hole through (fit the drill or reamer in the hole - set vertical aligned to the square).

Form a lead into the hole (opposite to popped end) - so as a pellet can drop in easily and settle about 1/8" deeper than the tap edge (use a taper pin reamer held in the wrench - or a small scraper) - de-burr - study the sketch.

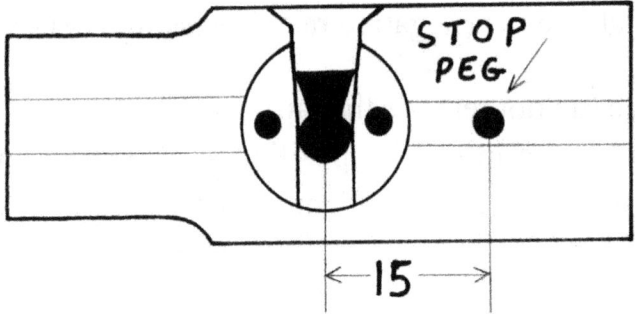

Drill the port hole out in stages so as a pellet can drop through easily then form a large countersink with a nice smooth finish - de-burr thoroughly so as the tap will slide in nicely and not get scored (needle file - scalpel point).

Clean thoroughly - assemble - inspect - if all is well the tap should slide in and turn smoothly - the bore hole should align with the port hole and you should be able to drop a pellet in easily - it should drop down and settle deep in the tap without it wanting to trap or jamb - study the sketch.

Fitting the lever - the idea is - you lift the lever - it hits a dead stop - at this point the tap bore is inline with the port hole - you drop a pellet in - it settles deep in the tap - you push the lever down - it hits a dead stop - at this point the tap bore is inline with the barrel bore - now - a spring loaded ball bearing locates in a detent (this is cut in the levers side) - it prevents the lever from flapping about.

Pop the hole for the stop peg - study the sketch - drill 3·3mm. into the airway - tap M.4 - de-burr - produce the stop peg (use an old allen screw) - saw off to leave 5mm. of thread - saw off to leave 4mm. of plain shank - use the junior hacksaw to cut a small screwdriver slot in the end - de-burr.

Clean all the parts thoroughly - assemble - fit the bore drill/reamer so as to set the tap in the exact closed position.

The lever is made from 3mm. or 1/8" thick ground flat stock - study the sketch - scribe the centerlines square to the top face - pop the center lightly - pop the two screw holes - set the dividers to scribe the 17·5mm. and 12·5mm. rad's. - scribe

the arm area - saw/grind so as to finish sharp and square on the scribes with the file - de-burr.

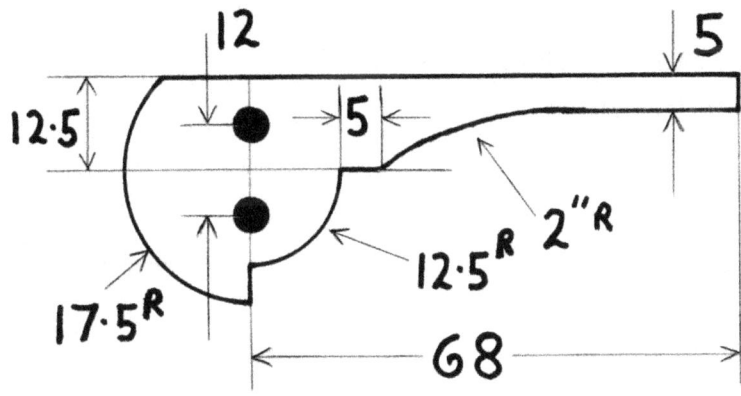

Drill the screw holes through 2·5mm. then 4mm. then countersink (same as the spring side sideplate) - de-burr - prepare two screws to suit - total length 13mm.

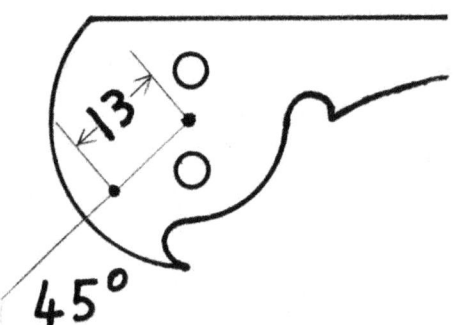

Cut the relief for the stop peg (3/16" chainsaw file) - start the rad. off then align for inspection (remember - the holes will become dead inline with the threaded holes just as soon as you reach the correct depth) - take care - study the sketch.

Set the tap in the open position - use the same technique so the tap will be fully open just as the lever hits the peg - take care - avoid overfile - study the sketch.

When all is well - scribe the 45° line through the center - pop the detent pilot - drill through 1/16" - de-burr - remove any scribe marks with fine emery - use the needle file to cut a tiny chamfer around all the edges - on both sides.

Heat the lever tip to bright red - hammer round a bar so as to cause the end to curl upwards and flare out - study the sketches - form a full rad. on the end of the flare (the cold anvil may cause the stock to harden - if so shape with the grinder or diamond file then polish with fine emery).

Assemble for inspection - see the lever is not binding (if need be - ward the tap housing with the file/emery strip so as the tap will turn smoothly) - set in the closed position with the drill/reamer aligning the bores - mount on parallels so as to spot the detent hole then dismantle.

Form the detent in the lever (use the 3·3mm. drill - take care look close - stop just before the drill point reaches full dia.) remove any burring with wet/dry.

Drill the ball hole through 2·5mm. then 3·3mm. - turn over - tap M.4 x 6mm. deep - de-burr - clean thoroughly.

Set the tap in the 3 jaw - form a small rad. on the outer shoulder then polish the face with wet/dry - study the cover photograph.

Set the tap aligned with the bore drill/reamer - use the fibre pen to mark the tap shoulder inline with the detent hole - remove - set in the vice so as the mark is vertical - use the 3/16" chainsaw file to cut a small notch in the shoulder (so as the grub screw will fit) - de-burr - clean all parts thoroughly - assemble - inspect.

Obtain a 1/8" ball bearing (cycle shop?) - obtain a suitable spring (old lighter?) - produce a slot head grub screw about 4mm. long (allen screw - junior hacksaw?) assemble - inspect with a pellet - it should operate just as described earlier - if all is well - dismantle and store the parts safely.

Pop the rivet holes - drill through 2·5mm. - de-burr - produce a scribing guide (stalk ·098 - head ·393) - scribe the two 5mm. rad's (on both sides of the tap) - study the sketch.

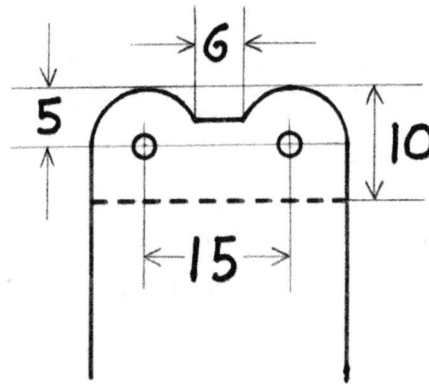

Set square in the milling machine vice so as to cut the two slots - set the spindle central to the taps width - lock the slide - use the 7mm. cutter to rough the sideplate slot to 9·7mm. deep.

Index to depth with a nice sharp cutter or slot drill that is the same size as the sideplate stock - finish in one steady pass - so as to ensure a good surface finish with nice sharp corners.

Set the spindle central to the taps depth - lock the slide - arm the spindle with a 6mm. cutter - sink down so as the slot corners are just touching on the rad. scribes (look closely - study the sketch).

Remove - de-burr - if all is well the tap should be a nice slide fit on the sideplate and the front of the sideplate should bed in the bottom of the slot.

Set at 45° so as to cut flats on the rad. scribes (take care - look close - less filing) - remove - finish sharp and square on the scribes with the file.

Use the needle file to cut a tiny chamfer on the rad's. outer edges (leave the slots inner edges crisp and sharp).

FITTING THE BARREL

The idea is - the loading tap is fixed to the sideplate with two precision rivets - the barrel is fixed to the loading tap with silver solder - the assembly is fixed to the mainframe with the hole 4 screw then the barrel is soft (lead) soldered to the mainframe to provide extra strength and rigidity.

Fit the tap to the sideplate - set the assembly in the machine vice (the barrel socket should be square to the back jaw) - mount the tap on a parallel - mount the sideplate on a parallel plus a 6mm. drill shank so as the assembly is lying flat (trap a flat plastic shim against the back jaw to protect the plates sharp corner).

See the sideplate is bedded square and the top and bottom faces are set flush - drill the rivet holes through 3/16" then ream 5mm. - remove - separate.

Chamfer the holes lightly on the hammer side - de-burr only on the lever side - clean thoroughly.

Produce two mild steel rivets - the shanks should be exactly 21mm. long - they should be parallel and a nice slide fit in the reamed holes - the heads should be 8mm. dia. and faced to exactly 2mm. thick - they should also have a 1mm. corner rad. - study the cover photograph - assemble - inspect.

(If using a rifled barrel - form a small chamfer leading into the bore - so as the pellet will leave the tap and then flow into the grooves smoothly).

Set the barrel bedded in the socket - set the assembly in the vice so as only the top quarter of the tap hole is visible and the barrel is vertical - heat so as to fill the joint with silver solder - overfill so as to form a nice internal rad. that blends to the barrel - let cool - remove flux with boiling water - tidy the joint with the half round needle file (if need be) - polish with fine emery.

Fit the sideplate with the hole 4 screw - form the angle on the mainframe so as the loading tap can bed flush and square - take care avoid overfile (try to get the angle so it beds to the barrel - this makes the soldering work easier) - the barrels centerline should be inline and parallel with the mainframes top face when the angle gets to the correct size - and both rivets should slide in smoothly - assemble to inspect as the angle forms (rough out on the grinder - using a 15mm. dia. barrel and filing at 45° should leave the top flat about 1/16" wide) - study the sketch.

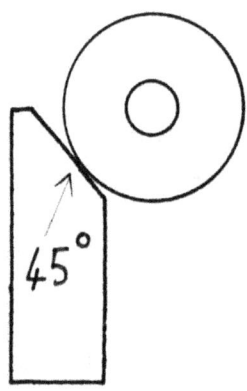

At this point - the surface finish and color required on the finished article should be considered - I would say that the finish achieved with the file and needle file are suited to this style of action - colouring with the blowlamp and the "cold blue" stuff from the gun shop is also quite adequate - in this department I am no expert - it seems there are many different ways to go about bluing metal parts - most of which require special chemicals that are not readily available in small quantities - or are not for sale to the general public - you may be expert in this department and have better ideas than mine - hereon I can only describe the simple route I took.

De-grease the loading tap (toothbrush - methylated spirits) - let dry - heat the entire tap so as to obtain a nice dark blue color that flows on to the start of the barrel (take care not to over-heat - this could melt the silver solder or distort the tap hole) - spray with W.D.40 just before completely cold - wipe clean and dry.

De-grease the sideplate - hang on a small nail set in the vice - heat to blue - W.D. 40 - clean (same as done with the tap) - blue the sight and its screw - assemble (put a drop of oil in the 3mm. thread).

Fit the sideplate to the tap with the O ring in position (set the barrel in the vice - push together - so as to fit the rivets in - from the hammer side).

Hammer the rivets just enough so as to prevent them from moving about - work on a smooth anvil - use a hammer with a smooth crown face - strike squarely - avoid over hammering - it could deform the 5mm. rad's. (see the rivet shoulders are bedded up tight - position on a thick 1/4" washer to knock up - if need be).

Set level in the vice so as to file the waste off - polish with the file/emery strip so as the area is smooth and flat (avoid removing metal from the tap hole edge) - re-cut the small rad. chamfers (if need be) - run the file/emery strip over the rivet heads (if need be) - clean thoroughly.

Use the needle file to cut a small chamfer on the mainframes sharp edges (forward of the trigger guard recess - running round to the firing pin bush) - so as the action will not be sharp to the touch.

Degrease with toothbrush/meths - hang - heat to blue all over - W.D. whilst still just warm - clean/dry (take care - avoid overheating).

Emery the 45° angle to bright - remove any oxide blue or scale on the adjacent barrel area - drop a blob of oil in the hole 4 thread - lock the sideplate in precise position (check faces are thoroughly clean - and all other screws align).

Grip the barrel in the vice - set so as to flood the joint with ordinary lead solder (see silver and lead soldering) - let cool - remove the flux with hot water (it is very corrosive) - tidy with a razor sharp wood chisel and wet/dry - if need be.

Blue the riveted area with "cold blue" I have only used "Abbey blu gel" and it did the job just fine (de-grease with meths/toothbrush - let dry - apply the gel with a cotton bud - scrub clean with toothbrush/meths - repeat and repeat until the color blends in with the blowlamp blue) - finish with toothbrush/meths and W.D.

Blue the tap lever - trigger guard and all fixing screws - W.D. - assemble (again - blob of oil in all threads - this will prevent the screws from seizing in).

THE FRONT SIGHT

The front sight is a steel blade - it is silver soldered to a brass base - the base is soft soldered to the barrel so it is not to difficult to adjust - the base blank should be about 1-1/2" long and 4mm. larger than the barrels O.D. - study the sketches.

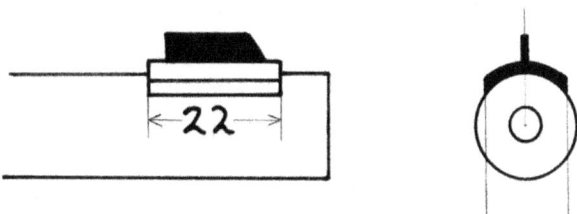

Set a brass bar in the 3 jaw so as to turn the end 25mm. down to being 4mm. larger than the barrels O.D. - face - drill/bore out to barrel dia. x 25mm. deep.

Set a scriber in the toolpost so as to mark a parallel centerline - put a tiny pop on the scribe - set the dividers to mark half the width of the base (to suit the barrel).

Set the toolpost scriber to the edges of the rad. scribes so as to mark the sides equal and parallel to the centerline (use the torch - look close) - study the sketch.

Use the toolpost scriber to mark the length (so the scribe is square) - set vertical in the vice so as to saw the back half off - then saw down the side scribes - set level so as to finish sharp on the side scribes with the file - study the sketch.

Saw/file to length (trap a small roller in the rad. so as to prevent distortion) - de-burr - align for inspection - if all is well the base should be 2mm. thick - it should bed to the barrel - it should also look symmetrical and square - with an accurate centerline.

Produce the blade (1/16" thick ground flat stock) - measure the distance from the top of the rear sight blade - to - the top of the barrel then deduct 2mm. to give you the correct height - study the sketch.

Fitting the blade (without distorting the base) - produce a thick wall tube about 1" long - it should be the same dia. as the barrel - it should have a small flat filed on the side (to prevent it rolling) - set the base on the tube - set the blade in position - set a block/blocks that is/are the same height as the assembly about 7" away - place a stout strip/bar bridging across so as to hold the blade in position - use the scriber point to fine tune - so as the blade is set looking symmetrical and vertical.

Heat so as to run a tiny bead of silver solder along the joint (touch the rod on the front edge - this should cause the solder to flow along the entire length - it should fill equally and evenly leaving the joint looking neat and tidy) - let cool - scald with boiling water to remove the flux - tidy with the round needle file (if need be).

Hold the base in position - the blades centerline should appear to cut through the center of the bore - if all is well grip the blade in the vice so as to tin the underside with soft lead solder.

Grip the barrel in the vice - see the sideplate is set vertical (hold a long rule or level against - for inspection) - clean/tin the joint area - study the sketch.

Position the sight - heat so it drops and beds (look from the front - use the scriber to adjust and hold - so as the blade settles and sets looking vertical).

Clean the base top and blade sides with a strip of fine emery folded over the end of a steel rule.

Leave any excess solder (the sight may require adjustment).

THE MAINSPRING

Most antique guns - some of them hundreds of years old still have their original mainsprings - many of them work just as well as they did on the day when they where first fitted - as said before - the action is reliant on the hammer and trigger mechanisms operating freely - so as the energy provided by the mainspring is not hindered - thus - not affecting the consistency of the firing cycle.

In the order of keeping the action looking sleek and simple - the spring/stop design is maintenance free and non adjustable - hence - the spring manufacture must be carried out meticulously (I am no world authority on springs or spring design - but - I was an apprentice toolmaker in a spring factory).

The first thing is to produce a flat spring steel blank (EN 45) - the best place to find spring steel that has not been hardened and tempered is of course an automotive spring makers - they all must have loads of offcuts - if they are all too far away the blank can be made from an old spring without any problems.

Use the angle grinder armed with a slitting wheel to produce a section that is larger than 5" x 1" - it must be thick enough to machine down to ·187 thick.

The blank must be annealed - this will make it soft enough to machine down to size - then it can be shaped with the hacksaw and file - it must be brought to bright red hot - all over - then it must cool slowly.

(Gas torch) - set the blank on - and leaning on other steelstock - steadily heat to bright red - or set the piece in a large wood fire - so long as it gets to bright red - all over - then it must be left it to cool in warmish air.

Set the piece on parallels in the milling machine vice - skim the faces with a nice sharp fly cutter - the blank should be ·187 thick - and flat - the faces should be polished with fine emery so the scribes will appear crisp and clear - study the actual shape - the arm should be a nice even taper - so it will flex like an eagles claw - or - fisherman's rod.

Produce an accurate scribing guide from a nice flat piece of sheet (this will make the scribing inspecting and modifying "easy work") - set the dividers to scribe the 8" rad. - saw/grind - finishing sharp and square on the scribe with the file.

Scribe the centerlines - pop the fixing hole - set the dividers to scribe the 8mm. and 12mm. rad's. - scribe the 1/4" ball (use the divider points to hold a suitable washer on the centerline then scribe round the hole) - the bottom of the ball and 8mm. rad. should be just above the edge of the blank - study the sketch.

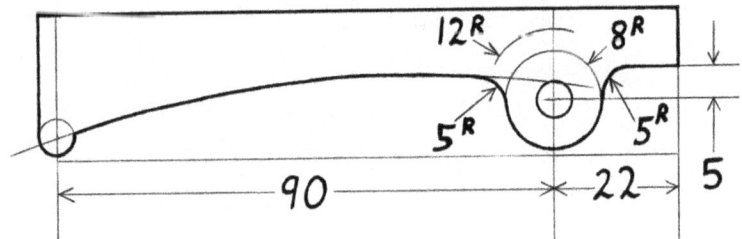

Scribe the stop flat - it is 5mm. above the fixing holes centerline - it is parallel with the blanks bottom edge - drill the fixing hole through 3mm. then 5mm. then 1/4" then countersink lightly on both sides - study the sketch.

Use the guide to scribe the bottom of the arm - the 8" rad. runs inline with the balls centerline - it runs inline with the fixing holes top edge - use the head on the trigger guards "rivet" guide to blend the arm and stop flat to the 8mm. rad. - study the sketch - saw/grind - allow for finishing sharp and square on the scribes with the file - see the arm merges sharply on the balls centerline - inspect the 8" rad. with the guide.

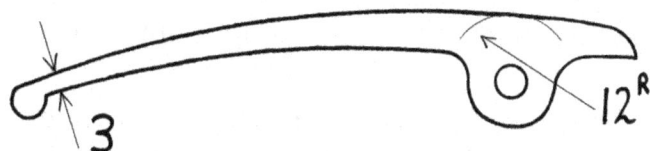

Mark the arm thickness close to the ball - use the guide to scribe the top of the arm - the 8" rad. clips the thickness mark - it clips the 12mm. rad. - saw out (a sharp 18 t.p.i. hacksaw blade should follow the curve) - grind close - finish sharp and square on the scribe with the file - inspect the 8" rad. with the guide - be certain the ball will bed in the links socket (align to inspect) - form a 5mm. rad. on the front/top edge - study the sketch - use the needle file to cut a tiny chamfer all round the edges - on both sides.

Now the spring must be "hardened" and then "tempered" - first it must be brought to bright red - all over (I tied a length of welding wire through the fixing hole then set it in a pile of hot embers in my wood stove) - if using the gas torch a small sheet steel enclosure may be required - so as to contain the flame and cause it to heat the entire arm evenly.

When the spring is bright red all over - it should be quickly removed from the heat and then quenched in oil (old engine oil will do the job just fine) - I lowered the spring in to a deep bucket of oil with the attached wire then swirled it around so it cooled quickly and evenly (do not consider using water - that would scrap all of the work ----- instantly).

The spring is now in a "brittle state" - it must be handled like a piece of glass - remove the wire - wipe clean and dry - the edges can be left black - the faces must be restored to a bright finish (set the spring on a flat wooden board - polish with fine emery) - wash in hot soapy water so as to thoroughly de-grease.

Take great care now - once the spring has been de-greased - it should not be touched with "bare fingers" - any slight surface contamination will disturb the "color run" process - set a nail sticking out from the vice - hang the spring from it (use only clean tissue paper when handling the spring - most important).

Now tempering - or - "blueing" - I used a modern gas blowlamp here - play the flame on the fixing hole area - watch for it turning to a dark straw color - then a nice deep blue - at this point - start to work the flame down the arm - causing the deep blue color to run down to the ball - watch carefully - take care don't rush the operation - when blued leave to slowly air cool - when completely cold spray with W.D. 40 - wipe dry - store safely.

In the factory - the tempering process is done in ovens with exact temperature control - under heat ---- the spring will snap like a carrot - over heat ---- the spring will just bend and lose its shape (in that case it is possible to bend back to form and repeat the harden/temper process - take care - avoid going down that road).

THE LAW

U.K. Law. Air rifle power limit --------

The air rifle, (Any calibre) Should not produce power that is over 12 foot pounds energy. Any air rifle that is set to produce power over that limit is classed as a firearm. Any person producing or owning an air rifle that is set to produce power over the legal limit is committing a criminal offence.

To set the rifles power level, a chronograph is required. This is an electronic device that accurately measures the speed of the fired projectile in feet per second. Use the mathematical equation below to calculate the foot pounds energy of the rifle.

(velocity (fps) X velocity (fps) X projectile weight (grains) / 450240 = ft/lbs.

Simplified ----

Multiply the speed of the projectile by itself - then multiply that answer by the weight of the projectile - then divide by 450240 - Then you have the foot pounds energy.

If the rifle was to be used set above the legal power limit - a firearm certificate from the police must be obtained FIRSTLY ----- This is most important.

Ignoring this could lead to imprisonment - the maker/owner would be in possession of an unlicensed firearm.

SETTING UP

Blue the mainspring link - the hammer and its pivot pin - set in position - fit the 3/32" pin - set the bars and brass washers in position.

Use the needle file to cut a small chamfer on the spring side sideplates sharp outer edges - so as the action will not be sharp to the touch - see all the screw heads are nice and smooth (file/emery strip) - blue the plate/screws - blue the top spacer and trigger pull (take care here).

Blob of oil in all 4mm. threads - set the sideplate on the pivot pins - slide the top spacer in - fit the top two screws - slide the front spacer in - fit the screw - tighten the screws to half a turn off nipped - set the hammer fully back - slide the trigger assembly in - fit the screw - lock all screws.

Blue the trigger guard and its screws - assemble (oil in threads) - cock - inspect.

Obtain two tough 1/4" U.N.F. hex. head bolts (local garage?) - the shanks should be 15mm. long - set in the lathe to form a slight dome on the heads (use the file - then polish with fine emery) - heat to blue - study the cover photograph.

The mainspring should be set so it holds the hammers face on the firing pin bush (this is only to prevent the hammer from rattling about) - once set it should not require further adjustment (provided the spring has been hardened and tempered correctly) - the job can be done without having to produce a special compressing tool - but care must be taken so as not to cause any damage to the parts.

Grip the barrel in the vice so as the mechanism is lying flat - set the hammer fully forward (touching on the bush) - fit the mainspring in position (lightly nipped) - be certain the stop bolt can be wound in easily with just the fingers.

Measure the distance from the spring flat - to - the edge of the stop bolt thread (fit the bolt - use drill shanks as feeler gauges) - calculate the stops exact dia.

Produce the stop (silversteel) - it should be ·200 thick - it should be flat - it should have a 1/4" hole through the center - it should be concentric and ·020 larger than the calculated measurement (face - turn - drill - part - de-burr).

Align the stop (it should not be possible to fit the bolt with the fingers) - use the Gordon grips to compress the spring just enough so as to cause the stop flat to lift slightly (bind the jaws with electrical tape or strips of lead - grip inline with the loading tap area - nip on the top corner of the spring arm/bottom corner of the mainframe) - this should enable the bolt to be screwed home with just the fingers.

(Do not be tempted to reach for the spanner - this will result in thread damage) - the spring tension need only cause the hammers face to rest on the bush - so the spring need only be flexed very slightly - look closely - take care here (in the case of error - produce another the stop) - when all is well lock the parts in position.

Charge the reservoir to 150 BAR - fit the firing pin - assemble - drop of thick oil on the trigger mechanism - cock by fanning the hammer back with the bottom of the palm (it's the safest and easiest way) - inspect with the chronograph.

For non F.A.C. use here in the U.K. it is likely that the power level may require adjustment - the best way to reduce the hammers blow strength is to feather the spring arm down slightly - use the guide and carbide scriber to position an accurate re-scribe on the arms top edge - use the grinder to work to the scribe - inspect with the chronograph - polish with the file/emery strip - re-cut the tiny chamfers with the oil stone or diamond file - touch up with "cold blue" when the correct power level is set.

Stick with one brand and weight of pellet so as not to cause a variation in the F.P.S. output - see the sight is set to shoot straight and level at about 35 yards (adjust the front sight - if need be) - remove any excess solder with a razor sharp wood chisel and wet/dry paper - finish the barrel and sight with the cold blue (don't seek perfection - a perfect bluing job would look totally wrong anyway).

I never set out to build a powerful airgun - reliability and the sleek appearance were of greater importance - for F.A.C. - or maximum power (which I have not explored) the valve design (as is) will have an optimum knock open setting - what I am trying to say is the blast will blow the ball down the barrel - the speed it will reach will be governed by the airway design and blast pressure - knocking the valve open over the optimum setting will only waste the stored air - there may be ways of upping the power level - I have no interested in that area - I think if you need an airgun of greater power - you will also need a greater action/valve design.

At this point - go shoot - shoot square - take care.

REMEMBER ---- Only cock and fire when a charged reservoir is attached.
REMEMBER ---- Charge ----100 BAR (min.) ---- 150 BAR (max.).
REMEMBER ---- Fan the hammer back with the bottom of the palm.
REMEMBER ---- Never store with a pellet in the tap.
REMEMBER ---- Always remove the reservoir before compressing the mainspring - this allows the hammer to move fully forward so the link is in its lowest position.
REMEMBER ---- Always compress the mainspring when fitting or removing the stop - this will prevent damaging the U.N.F. threads.
REMEMBER ---- Always use thick tape or lead on the grip jaws when compressing the mainspring - this will prevent damaging the spring/mainframe.
REMEMBER ---- Always compress the mainspring and remove the stop before stripping the action.
REMEMBER ---- Most fellows that make or mess with airguns tend to modify or adapt from other makers ideas - very few will design and build from scratch - When my son was knee high I went off to the shed to make an airgun - Later - I came back with this design - At this point - my son had grown to 6 feet tall - and was managing an estate agents office.

SILVER AND LEAD SOLDERING

Silver solder is basically a low temperature braze - I say low temperature - the joint still needs to be bordering on dull red before it will flow nicely - the operations on this project are best done with a clean burning flame from the oxy-acet. welding torch - or if careful - the short cutting torch - I use a "Rothenberger Superfire" brazing torch - but it must be used in conjunction with the hotter burning "Mapp Gas" this is a plumber's type blowlamp - the only one I have seen capable of producing the heat required for doing this type of job.

Always purchase silver solder together with the correct powder type flux from a good engineer's merchant - make sure there is no grease or oxide in the joint (methylated spirit is a good de-greaser) - check the joint it is set right and level.

Play the flame on the joint so as it heats the parts equally - watch for the steel parts turning blue - at this point dip the rod into the flame then into the flux - this will cause a small amount of powder to stick.

Now touch the rod in the joint (don't let the flame melt the rod) - if you are close to temperature the powder will liquefy and spread - see it coats the joint - keep the heat on and look close - as the heat increases the acid in the flux will react - this will cause the surfaces to clean - the rod will flow and bond - but at this stage the joint will be bordering on dull red hot.

At this point - position the flame so as only the rod tip melts - avoid large blobs - these will usually cause trouble - re-flux when building up or moving on - this temperature band is critical - now the flux will clean and the rod should flow on contact.

The solder will always want to flow to the hottest area - but firstly the flux must react and clean so it will bond - keep the flux close to hand then you can re-apply quickly.

Overheating can burn the nature out of the flux - this results in a black surface crusting - heating with a sooty flame will also cause crusting - the fluxes natural reaction will not remove this - and the solder will not flow - you must stop - let cool - file or scrape thoroughly clean then continue - overheat can also cause the solder to boil - this will leave its surface looking rough or bubbly.

Leave joints to air cool - scald with boiling water to remove the flux.

The ancient art of lead soldering - at this I am no "Black Belt" but I can explain how to make a reasonable looking job - many years ago soldered joints where commonplace as are the glued joints of today - now I can only relate lead solder to printed circuit boards and plumbers pipes - on this project the solder work need not be neat - as the joints can be scraped to shape when they are cold - it is more important that they are bonded and filled - so as to make the shaping work simple - I can only describe working with ordinary plumbers lead solder - I have never used the new "lead free" type - required is some "Bakers soldering fluid" and a gas blowlamp that will produce a small flame with a sharp blue cone - so as to focus the heat ----- I will explain how I fill a long joint.

Again - make sure there is no grease or oxide in the joint - see the parts are set firmly so they will not move - see the joint is butted up tight and lying level - wherever possible - firstly the joint must be covered with a bonded coat of solder - this stage is called "tinning" - it is the most important part of the operation.

Focus the flame on the start point so it heats the joint evenly - dip the rod in the fluid - remove the flame - touch the rod in the joint - listen for the fluid boiling and hissing - this will prove you are close to temp.

Keep heat spread to an absolute minimum - at all times.

Heat slightly - dip - remove the flame - touch on - look for the flux cleaning the surfaces on contact - REMEMBER - remove the flame and re-dip every time you touch on.

Heat slightly - now look for the solder melting on contact - see it is bonding to both halves of the joint - don't attempt to fill the joint instantly - concentrate on the tinning process - move the tinning coat on then return to fill the joint.

Now let the workpiece melt the rod - take care to keep flame application minimal - overheat will cause the solder to flow into un-tinned areas - hence - a lead joint that is not fully bonded to the workpiece.

In the event of an area not wanting to tin or fill - stop - let cool - use the scraper to clean the area meticulously then continue - there is no fear of causing damage or ruination to the parts.

Let joints air cool then wash/scrub thoroughly with water - so as to remove all traces of the flux - it is very corrosive.

MATERIALS

Reservoir -- (I would recommend good second hand) --
Try -- diving shops that sell used equipment -- adverts in diving magazines -- computer auction sites -- car boot -- local sub-aqua clubs --

Bright drawn mild steel –
Try -- any steel stockholders that sells off-cuts -- model engineering supplies -- light engineering works --

H E 30 aluminium -- CZ 121 brass -- Stainless steel –
Try -- non ferrous steel stockholders that sell off-cuts -- light engineering works -- model engineering supplies --

Nylon -- Phosphor bronze --
Try -- model engineering supplies --

Barrel tubing (hydraulic) -- O rings -- B.S.P. connectors -- Dowty washers –
-- hydraulic and pneumatic supplies -- hydraulic engineers --

Barrel (used - rifled) –
scrap bin at any local gun shop -- car boot -- computer auction sites --

Barrel (new - rifled) –
T. W. Chambers - airgun spares" Ross-Shire Scotland --

Solder -- Flux -- Ground flat stock -- Machine screws -- Silversteel –
Engineers merchants -- model engineering supplies -- fastener stockists --